A CITY FROM
THE DAWN OF HISTORY

Erbil in the Cuneiform Sources

John MacGinnis

Chevron

Oxbow Books
Oxford & Philadelphia

Published in the United Kingdom in 2014 by
OXBOW BOOKS
10 Hythe Bridge Street, Oxford OX1 2EW

and in the United States by
OXBOW BOOKS
908 Darby Road, Havertown, PA 19083

Paperback Edition: ISBN 978-1-78297-797-1
Digital Edition: ISBN 978-1-78297-798-8

A CIP record for this book is available from the British Library

Printed in the United Kingdom by Short Run Press, Exeter

For a complete list of Oxbow titles, please contact:

UNITED KINGDOM

Oxbow Books
Telephone (01865) 241249, Fax (01865) 794449
Email: oxbow@oxbowbooks.com
www.oxbowbooks.com

Oxbow Books is part of the Casemate Group

UNITED STATES OF AMERICA

Oxbow Books
Telephone (800) 791–9354, Fax (610) 853–9146
Email: queries@casemateacademic.com
www.casemateacademic.com/oxbow

Cover illustration – Watercolour illustrating an example of glazed bricks, from the temple of Aššur in Assur (Andrae 1923, Plate VI)

Title page illustration – Nabonidus Chronicle, recording Cyrus the Great passing near Erbil through the territory of his Median allies en-route to invade Urartu in 547 BC (see p. 118) British Museum, London – BM 35382

Contents

Maps

Foreword

The study and conservation of archaeology and heritage, so as to demonstrate previously unknown historical facts without negatively affecting other people's rights, is a national obligation. The starting point of the Ministry of Culture and Youth has been a sense of responsibility for providing information on the rich and ancient history and culture of the Kurdistan Region. With the special guidance of H.E. Dr. Kawa M. Shakir, Minister of Culture and Youth of the Kurdistan Regional Government, we decided to commission this book to present some of the historical facts and events illustrated by sources existing in the museums and archives of other nations which are relevant to the history of the Kurdish nation, facts which successive central regimes tried hard to obliterate and distort.

To achieve this we commissioned Dr. John MacGinnis of the University of Cambridge McDonald Institute of Archaeological Research and Mr. David Michelmore, coordinator of the Erbil Citadel Conservation Master Plan, to research the archaeological and archival sources of other nations with regard to materials relating to the history and civilisation of Kurdistan and of Erbil in particular – Hawler, to give it its Kurdish name, being one of the oldest inhabited cities in the world, a gateway to history and the capital of the Kurdistan Region.

We present the results of Dr. MacGinnis' research, which has identified nearly 300 documents and sources dating from the Third Millennium BC to the conquest by Alexander the Great at the Battle of Arbela. The documents show that there were many wars and battles in the region, especially in and around Erbil, and unfortunately the victims of such conflicts were the people of Kurdistan.

We will live to participate with other nations living on this globe to enrich human civilization and to spread the values of virtue, knowledge, and wisdom.

Kanan Mufti
General Director
Ministry of Culture and Youth – Kurdistan Regional Government

Preface

This project of collecting and assessing the evidence for the history of Erbil as documented in the cuneiform sources originated in the context of the work carried out for and by the High Commission for Erbil Citadel Revitalisation (HCECR), the authority constituted by the Kurdistan Regional Government (KRG) and supported by UNESCO in order to develop and implement the regeneration of the urban centre of Erbil. This resulted in the evolution of the Master Plan for Erbil, a comprehensive strategy for regenerating the historic city through a co-ordinated approach comprising the documentation, preservation, presentation and utilisation of the architectural heritage. Necessarily, addressing the archaeological heritage has formed an important part of this plan and in accordance with this an archaeological assessment of the citadel mound was carried out early in 2009. In addition to making a number of recommendations for addressing the archaeological heritage of the city, that assessment also recommended a comprehensive collection of the information preserved in cuneiform sources pertaining to the history of Erbil. The Ministry of Culture and Youth of the Kurdistan Region of Iraq therefore commissioned the collection of the cuneiform sources through the Consultancy for Conservation and Development Ltd, which has been responsible for the preparation of the Master Plan for the Citadel. In the event this research turned up nearly three hundred cuneiform texts making reference to Erbil over a timeframe stretching from the late third millennium to the mid first millennium BC.

I would like to take this opportunity to thank the many people who have helped and supported this project. First and foremost I would like to express my deep appreciation to H.E. Kawa Shakir Mahmoud, Minister of Culture and Youth of the Kurdistan Regional Government, for his vision in commissioning this study; to Kanan Mufti, General Director in the Ministry of Culture and Youth; to Sami Alkhoja (UNESCO Programme Officer for the Kurdistan Region of Iraq) and to David Michelmore (Consultancy for Conservation and Development): without the support of these people this undertaking would not have happened.

I would also like to thank my colleagues in the field of Assyriology who have so generously given of their time and shared knowledge and expertise with respect to specialised areas of research: Heather Baker, Maria Giovanna Biga, Marco Bonechi, Grant Frame, Douglas Frayne, Jaume Llop, Mikko Luuko, Stefan Maul, Wiebke Meinhold, Jamie Novotny, Simo Parpola, Nicholas Postgate, Karen Radner, Gonzalo Rubio, Piotr Steinkeller, Adam Stone, Greta van Buylaere, Frans van Koppen and Magnus Widell. Their generosity has greatly contributed to the thoroughness and accuracy of the final text and is deeply appreciated.

I would also like to express my thanks to Narmin Ali, Béatrice André-Salvini, Vera Bulgurlu, Stafford Clarry, John Curtis, Amira Eidan al-Dhahab, Elisabeth Fontan, Zeynep Kızıltan, Konstantinos Kopanias, Maria Grazia Masetti-Rouault, David Michelmore, Anne Mollenhauser, Nicholas Postgate, Julian Reade, Jason Ur and Dirk Wicke for help with the illustrations. David Michelmore prepared the final text for printing. Amin al Mohamad, Paula Ion, Muhammed Nureddin, René Turner, Manhal Shaya and Jason Ur assisted with editing the maps and images which illustrate the text.

I would also like to express my deep appreciation to Clare Litt of Oxbow Books for accepting the work for publication and to all the staff at Oxbow Books for the care and attention with which they have steered it into print.

Last but decidedly not least I would like to record my deep appreciation to Chevron in Iraq for the generous subvention which made the publication of this work possible.

To all the above I extend my profound thanks and gratitude.

John MacGinnis
McDonald Institute for Archaeological Research
Cambridge

Abbreviations

AfO	*Archiv für Orientforschung*
AJAH	*American Journal of Ancient History*
AoF	*Altorientalische Forschungen*
AOAT	*Alter Orient und Altes Testament*
AUCT	*Andrews University Cuneiform Texts*
BaF	*Baghdader Forschungen*
BaM	*Baghdader Mitteilungen*
BIN	*Babylonian Inscriptions in the Collection of J B Nies*
Bi.Or.	*Bibliotheca Orientalis*
CHEU	*Contribution à l'Histoire Économique d'Umma*
CT	*Cuneiform Texts from Babylonian Tablets in the British Museum*
CTN	*Cuneiform Texts from Nimrud*
JCS	*Journal of Cuneiform Studies*
JNES	*Journal of Near Eastern Studies*
JSS	*Journal of Semitic Studies*
JTS	*Jewish Theological Seminary*
KAR	*Keilschrifttexte aus Assur Religiösen Inhalts*
KAV	*Keilschrifttexte aus Assur Verschiedenen Inhalts*
LAS	*Letters from Assyrian Scholars*
LKA	*Literarische Keilschrifttexte aus Assur*
MARV	*Mittelassyrische Rechts- und Verwaltungsurkunden*
MDOG	*Mitteilungen des Deutschen Orientgesellschaft*
MEE	*Materiali Epigrafici di Ebla*
MVN	*Materiali per il Vocabulario Neosumerico*
OECT	*Oxford Editions of Cuneiform Texts*
Or.Ant.	*Oriens Antiquus*
OIP	*Oriental Institute Publications*

OLA	Orientalia Lovaniensia Analecta
PDT	Die Puzriš-Dagan Texte der Istanbuler Archäologischen Museen
PKTA	Parfümrezepte und Kultische Texte aus Assur
RA	Revue d'Assyriologie
RIMA	Royal Inscriptions of Mesopotamia, Assyrian Periods
RlA	Reallexicon der Assyriologie
SAA	State Archives of Assyria
SAAB	State Archives of Assyria Bulletin
SAAS	State Archives of Assyria Series
SAT	Sumerian Archival Texts
StAT	Studien zu den Assur-Texten
STT	Sultan Tepe Texts
TCL	Textes Cunéiformes du Louvre
TCS	Texts from Cuneiform Sources
TCTI	Tablettes Cuéeiformes de Telloh au Musée d'Istanbul
TIM	Texts in the Iraq Museum
VS	Vorderasiatische Schriftdenkmäler
WVDOG	Wissentschaftliche Veröffentlichungen der Deutschen Orientgesellschaft
ZA	Zeitschrift für Assyriologie

Introduction

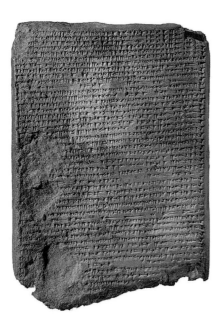

The city of Erbil lies at the foot of the piedmont of the Zagros mountains in a strategic position which made it a natural gateway between Iran and Mesopotamia. At the same time its command of the rich alluvial plains to the west ensured a flourishing agricultural base; the emergence of a city in this location was inevitable.

Erbil now claims to be one of the oldest continually inhabited cities in the world, and not without reason: archaeological surface survey has indeed produced potsherds dating back to the Ubaid period (*ca.* 5500–4000 BC). This combination of prolonged occupation and strategic location marks out Erbil as an exceptional site. Within the

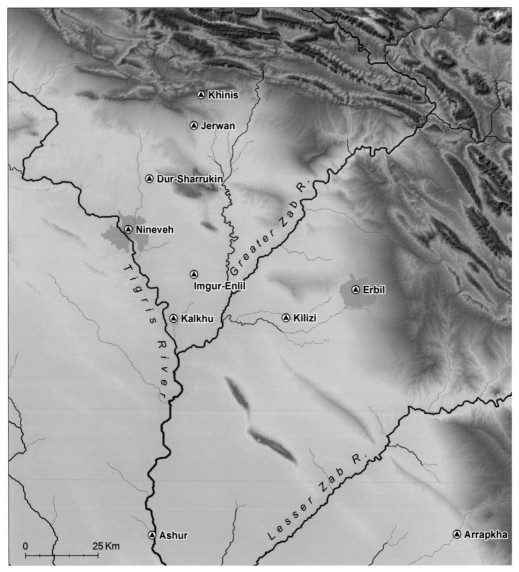

The location of Erbil in north-east Mesopotamia between the Great and Little Zab rivers (courtesy Jason Ur).

context of ancient Mesopotamian civilisation there can be no doubt that it will have been one of the most important urban centres. Nevertheless, archaeological research of the remains has been limited. In the nineteenth century the early explorers of Assyrian archaeology passed through but their priorities lay elsewhere, whilst in the twentieth century a mixture of different research agendas and later inaccessibility combined to ensure that the mound of Erbil was never the target of a focused campaign. With the advent of the twenty-first century, however, the prospects look rather better. Scholarly interest in northeastern Iraq has been awakened and the logistic and political conditions are more favourable. Three archaeological assessments of the mound have been conducted, two in 1997 and 2010 focusing on surface survey and remote sensing[1] and one in 2009 evaluating the significance of the remains within their historical context and evaluating how to approach archaeological investigations within the existing topography.[2] The possibility of the citadel mound of Erbil being the target of the level of major fieldwork which it so richly merits now looks decidedly more real. In these circumstances the time seems ripe to gather together and evaluate the ancient sources on the city. This work is dedicated to the cuneiform sources.

Cuneiform writing

After a long and interesting prehistory, writing finally emerged in Mesopotamia a little before 3,000 BC.[3] At first pictographic, the method of writing on clay with a triangular reed soon led to the evolution of the true cuneiform (wedge-shaped) script. This script was then in use until the first century AD, a period of over three thousand years. Over this immense time span the orthographics and utilisation of cuneiform underwent constant changes. From an initially logographic base the script rapidly became predominantly phonetic, evolving into the "mixed script" utilising syllabic signs, logograms and determinatives typical and characteristic of all primary writing systems. Although the determinatives remained relatively stable, the use of logograms varied greatly in different periods and places while the phonetic values of signs evolved continually. The physical appearance of the signs also evolved, generally becoming smaller and less complex over the centuries. The actual number of signs in normal use also gradually decreased. With regard to what the writing was used for, this also was continually evolving. From the origins as an administrative tool, cuneiform writing came to be used for letters, contracts, royal inscriptions, lexical texts,

1. Novacek 2007. Preliminary surface survey utilising GPR took place in 2010, see Colliva 2011.

2. MacGinnis 2009.

3. See Walker 1987 for an excellent survey on the history and development of the cuneiform writing system. For general surveys of the archaeology and history of ancient Iraq see Roux 1993 and Foster & Foster 2009.

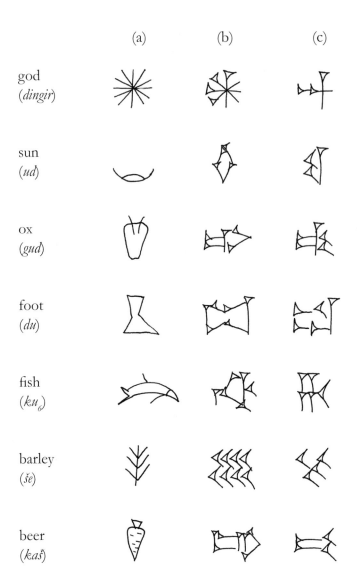

	(a)	(b)	(c)
god (*dingir*)			
sun (*ud*)			
ox (*gud*)			
foot (*du*)			
fish (*ku₆*)			
barley (*še*)			
beer (*kaš*)			

Development of cuneiform signs

The table shows a number of signs

(a) as they started out as pictographs in the fourth millennium,

(b) as they appear in cuneiform in the late third/early second millennium, and

(c) as they appear in the first millennium. The god sign depicts a star. When read as /du/ the foot sign means "to go".

omen texts, literature, prayers, rituals, commentaries, mathematical and astronomical texts and so on. Then the decline set in. The fall of the Assyrian empire in the closing years of the seventh century BC resulted in the rapid disappearance of cuneiform writing in the north. In the south the process of cessation was more gradual. Following the end of the Neo-Babylonian empire (539 BC), cuneiform continued as a thriving medium for about two generations, after which here too it began to fall away. In both the north and the south the process was in any case already set in train by the infiltration of Arameans into Mesopotamia and the rise of Aramaic as the major spoken language of the region. By the Hellenistic period the use of cuneiform was essentially restricted to the temples, where scribal schools kept alive the literary tradition while continuing to utilise the script in administration. By the Parthian period the chief use of cuneiform tablets was in astronomical texts: the latest know cuneiform text is an astronomical almanac dated to 74–75 AD.

The language for which the writing system was originally invented was almost certainly Sumerian but from the latter centuries of the third millennium it was adopted for writing Akkadian, the other major language of ancient Mesopotamia. Traditionally Akkadian has been divided into two principal dialects, Assyrian in the north and Babylonian in the south, but the reality is that the picture is more complex, at any rate in the earlier periods. In the fullness of time the Mesopotamian cuneiform writing system was also employed for writing a number of other languages: these include Hittite, Hurrian, and Urartian. In other cases, Ugaritic and Old Persian, it served as the inspiration for new writing systems which are cuneiform in appearance but have no detailed relation on the level of individual signs.

Chronology

The periods in which the cuneiform (and pre-cuneiform) writing system was used in Mesopotamia are as follows:

Uruk	4000 – 3000 BC
Early Dynastic	3000 – 2334 BC
Akkadian	2334 – 2193 BC
Gutian	2193 – 2120 BC
Ur III	2120 – 2004 BC
Old Assyrian/Old Babylonian	2004 – 1595 BC
Middle Assyrian/Middle Babylonian	1595 – 1000 BC
Neo-Assyrian/Neo-Babylonian	1000 – 612 BC

Neo-Babylonian Empire	612 – 539 BC
Achaemenid	539 – 330 BC
Hellenistic/Seleucid	330 – 126 BC
Parthian	126 BC – 224 AD

As will be readily appreciated, for the earlier part of this scheme the dates are approximate. This is for three different reasons: (1) for the earlier periods the dates really come from archaeology rather than texts and are therefore tied to archaeological methods of dating; (2) at times of fragmentation changes in dynasties happened in different parts of the land at different times; and (3) uncertainties in the historical chronology. The situation for the latter can be summarised as follows:

First Millennium

In the first millennium there is no particular problem with chronology: dates can generally be assigned to the correct year.

Late Second Millennium

For the late second millennium, which is to say the Middle Assyrian/Middle Babylonian periods, we cannot be so exact. Constructing the chronology of this period is a complex problem involving the collation of data from Assyrian and Babylonian chronicles, historical inscriptions and administrative texts as well as comparisons with external (e.g. Hittite and Egyptian) sources. A final resolution of these problems has not yet been achieved although the degree of accuracy is slowly improving. As a rule of thumb it is currently possible to suggest dates for the reigns of the Middle Assyrian kings with an accuracy of plus or minus 10 years: in this work the dates for these kings are taken from Freydank 1991 pp. 188–189. However the picture remains more complicated than that as texts were actually dated by the yearly eponym (*limu*). In numerous cases we do not know to which reign an eponym should be assigned, and even when we do know the position in the chronology of that reign is often unclear.

Late Third Millennium/Early Second Millennium

For the late third and early second millennia the picture is even more complicated. There is as yet no generally agreed proposal for anchoring the dates of this period. Internally the chronology forms a coherent block from the rise of the Ur III empire (under Utu-hegal) through to the fall of Babylon (under Samsu-Ditana), although there are innumerable complications caused by the fragmentation of Babylonia prior to Hammurapi. This is a span of approximately 525 years. Attempts to fix this span in time have not so far succeeded. For many years faith was put in the so called "Venus Tablet of Ammi-Saduqa", a record of sightings of the planet Venus. As Venus has a cycle of 56/64 years it was believed that one of three proposals would be correct: a Long Chronology (placing the fall of Babylon in 1659 BC), a Middle Chronology (fall of Babylon in 1595 BC) and a Short Chronology (fall of Babylon in 1531 BC). In the absence of conclusive evidence otherwise, many scholars settled on the Middle Chronology as a working compromise; the dates for this period given below are taken from this. More recently however the validity of the entire system has been questioned. A reappraisal of the evidence undertaken by a joint team from Ghent, Chicago and Harvard, taking into account both astronomical and archaeological evidence, came to the conclusion that local factors meant that the data had to be evaluated within an 8 year cycle and in fact came to the conclusion that the fall of Babylon can be dated to 1499 BC.[4] Although this date is not yet in general acceptance, it is true to say that to many scholars a shorter framework is increasingly looking more plausible. Nevertheless, it is still not yet possible to give absolute dates for this time period.

Overview of the sources

Having established the framework in which we are dealing, let us now review the nature and distribution of the cuneiform sources at our disposal.

Uruk Period (4000–3000 BC)

This is when writing was emerging in Mesopotamia. The texts from this time are administrative together with associated lexical lists. There are no known references to Erbil from this time and indeed it would be surprising if there were. It is however possible that such texts will have been generated in Erbil and may one day be found by excavation.

Early Dynastic Period (3000–2334 BC)

The same holds for the Early Dynastic period: no texts referring to Erbil are currently known but it is to be expected that with excavation this could change.

Akkadian Period (2334–2193 BC)

This is when Erbil enters history. Erbil is mentioned first in some documents from Ebla dating to shortly before the destruction of that city, contemporary with the early Akkadian period in Mesopotamia. The fact that large parts of Mesopotamia were in fact brought under the control of the Akkadian administration means that it is quite conceivable that references to Erbil may one day come to light in texts from elsewhere.

---

4. Gasche et al. 1998: pp. 72–73 for the evaluation of the Venus Tablet.

Gutian Period (2193–2120 BC)

By the reign of Šar-kali-šarri, the fifth king of the Dynasty of Sargon, the Akkadian empire was falling apart.[5] The territory of Akkad was fragmented, in part overrun by the Guti, a people who by the Old Babylonian period were seated in the mountainous region northeast of the lower Tigris, but who in the third millennium may have been localised in the mid-Euphrates area and /or northern Babylonia. The chronology and events of this period are very unclear. Erbil is mentioned in an inscription of the Gutian king Erridu-Pizir as an objective of a military campaign. This inscription is written in Akkadian.

Ur III (2120–2004 BC)

The expulsion of the Gutians by Utu-hegal led to the foundation of the Ur III empire which at its maximum extent constituted a multinational state ruling the greater part of Mesopotamia. It is not known whether or not Erbil had regained its independence from the Guti but it was in any case taken by both Shulgi and Amar-Sin and incorporated within the empire. The year names for Shulgi year 45 and Amar-Sin 02 refer to these events. In addition to this the city is referred to in a votive inscription from the time of Šu-Sin and in a number of administrative texts. These texts are written in Sumerian.

Old Assyrian/Old Babylonian[6] (2004–1595 BC)

There are two known references to Erbil from this time, both royal inscriptions, stelae of Dadusha and Shamshi-Adad. Both these inscriptions deal with the same joint campaign which these kings conducted in the northeast of Mesopotamia. Erbil at this time was part of the kingdom of Qabra and is likely to have been home to an indigenous temple and/or palace administration. An indication of what this may have been like is given by the tablets from Shemshara (on the Lower Zab) which do stem from the palace administration of an outlying regional kingdom of just this time.[7] Both stelae are written in Akkadian.

5. The Akkadian dynasty did in fact linger on for another forty years or so; the last king of the dynasty that we know of is Šu-Turul (2168–2154 BC) though there is at least one king, Li-lu-ul-DAN (see Frayne 1993 p. 218) whom we cannot place and it cannot be ruled out there may have been further petty successors whose inscriptions have not yet been recovered.

6. This period in question might equally be labelled Old Babylonian or Old Assyrian - the former because the events involved fit into the history of the region recorded in sources written in Old Babylonian, the latter because the region is later to become an unquestionable part of Assyria. The distinction is to some extent artificial and until sources are recovered from Erbil itself the matter is somewhat academic.

7. See Eidem 1992. Eidem and Laessoe 2001.

Middle Assyrian (1595–1000 BC)

With the Middle Assyrian period both the quantity and variety of sources at our disposal increase. Erbil is mentioned in three royal inscriptions, a votive inscription and approximately forty-five administrative texts. For the first time we are able to formulate something more than a one-dimensional image of the city. These texts are written in Akkadian.

Neo-Assyrian (1000–612 BC)

In the Neo-Assyrian period there is a huge increase in the range and quantity of the sources and the detail of information they provide. The sources include chronicle entries, royal inscriptions of seven different kings, oracular pronouncements, reports on divination, hymns, a cultic commentary, a votive inscription and altogether over 150 letters and administrative texts. Together these texts cover campaigns and victory celebrations; building work and rites in the principal temple of Ištar of Arbail in both Arbail (the Egašankalamma) as well as her countryside shrine at Milkia (the Egaledinna), together with information on royal donations, temple staff, offerings and rituals; the construction of a canal bringing water to the city; provincial administration including military organisation, the receipt of tribute and taxes, and the sending of dues to the temple of Aššur; and loans, contracts and records of judicial decisions. These texts are all written in Akkadian. We also have the first surviving depiction of the city in the form of sculptured reliefs from the North Palace and the Southwest Palace of Nineveh as well as representations of Ištar of Arbail herself on seals and amulets and on a stele from Til Barsip.

Bronze amulet of Ishtar of Arbail. The goddess stands on her vehicle, a lion, with her face turned towards the onlooker. A worshipper stands in front of the image. Other representations of the Ishtar cult statue show her looking straight ahead, as was almost certainly the case in reality (British Museum, London – BM 119437).

Neo-Babylonian Empire (612–539 BC)

The Neo-Babylonian Chronicle mentions that Cyrus crossed with his army below Erbil at the outset of his campaign in 547 BC. Apart from this there are no known references to Erbil in the Neo-Babylonian sources. As this is a time from which tens of thousands of administrative documents survive, this very silence suggests that the city did not form part of the Neo-Babylonian empire. The chronicle is written in Akkadian.

Achaemenid (539–330 BC)

Darius' inscription at Behistun records that he hunted down and impaled the rebel Shitrantakhma in Erbil (the Behistun inscription itself is trilingual, with versions in Akkadian, Old Persian and Elamite, and the text was also disseminated in Aramaic). There is one reference to Erbil in Akkadian administrative texts, in addition to which there are some unpublished citations which may refer to the city in administrative records from Persepolis written in Elamite; Erbil is also mentioned in the "Passport of Nehtihor", an official permit written on leather in Aramaic.

Hellenistic/Seleucid (330–126 BC)

Guagamela, where Alexander the Great defeated Darius III, was located in the plains northwest of Erbil and Alexander briefly visited the city after his victory before taking the road to Babylon. Although Alexander does appear in cuneiform texts of the time, including a reference to his entering Babylon, there are no known references to Erbil in the cuneiform documentation from this time.

Parthian (126 BC– 224 AD)

There are no known references to Erbil in the cuneiform texts from this period.

To summarise, there are a number of references to Erbil in Eblaite and Sumerian administrative texts of Akkadian and Ur III date and hundreds of references in Akkadian texts from the second and first millennia. Remarkably, only two of these inscriptions appear to have actually come from Erbil and even one of these is questionable. The votive statuette of Šamši-bel was evidently dedicated to Ištar in the Egašankalamma but actually found near lake Urmia whither it had presumably been taken as booty. This leaves the inscription of Ashurbanipal K891 as the sole cuneiform text which may have actually been found in Erbil and even this attribution is based on a note accompanying the original publication which is open to interpretation. There are a handful of references in unpublished Elamite texts from Persepolis. In Old Persian the city only appears in the corresponding version of the inscription at Behistun. There are no references in Hittite, Hurrian, Urartian or Ugaritic sources.

The name of Erbil

Over this period of cuneiform documentation the rendering of the city's name progresses from Irbilum in the Ebla texts, to Urbilum in the Ur III sources, to Urbēl in the Old Babylonian sources and on to Arbail in the Middle and Neo-Assyrian sources. The understanding that the name means "(city of) four gods" is an erroneous folk etymology deriving from a literal interpretation of the fact that from the Middle Assyrian period onward the city's name could be written using the cuneiform signs for "four" and "god". But this writing is simply a scribal shorthand as the signs are actually being used for their phonetic contents: in Akkadian "four" is *erbe* (or *arba*) and "god" is *il(u)*, hence a way of writing Erbil (Arbail).

We turn now to a more detailed analysis of what these sources have to say.

Writing Erbil *in cuneiform*

Due to the workings of the cuneiform writing system there are numerous different ways of writing the name of the city, furthermore this developed over time due to (1) the evolving pronunciation of the name, (2) changes in the usage of signs and (3) changes in the way individual signs were written. The four examples here span the late third to the early first millennium. In detail:

(a) **late third millennium**: *ur-bí-lum^{ki}* (from the Ur III text CT 32, 26)
  Phonetic spelling of the name of the city followed by the sign KI, a determinative used for both countries and large cities. The writing also has the Akkadian nominative ending – *um*; it is not known whether or not this was actually pronounced.

(b) **early second millennium**: *ur-bi-el^{ki}* (from the Stele of Dadusha, Old Babylonian)
  Phonetic spelling of the name of the city followed by the sign KI, a determinative used for both countries and large cities.

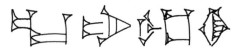

(c) **late second millennium**: ^{uru}*Ar-ba-il* (from the Middle Assyrian text KAJ 178).
  Phonetic spelling of the name of the city preceded by the sign URU, the determinative for cities.

(d) **mid first millennium**: ^{uru}4–DINGIR (from the Neo-Assyrian text SAAB 2 72).
  This writing consists of the city determinative URU followed by the sign for the number 4 and the sign for god. This is a rebus writing: as "four" is *arba* in Akkadian and "god" is *il*, the combination can be used to write the name Arbail. This writing has given rise to the view that the name of Erbil means "city of four gods". This is a later folk etymology and is wrong.

Historical Analysis

Erbil in the Gutian Period

Following some references to messengers going to Erbil in texts from Ebla, Erbil really enters history in an inscription of the Gutian king Erridu-Pizir, who reports attacking the city along with Simirrum and Lullubum. It has been suggested that Ur-bilum in fact lay within the state of Lullubum but this is far from certain. Nirišhuha, the name of the city ruler of Urbilum given in the inscription, is Hurrian and this may be taken as evidence that the population of Urbilum at that time was Hurrian or at least included a Hurrian component. The area where the Guti dwelt in the Zagros mountains corresponds to some extent with the area now inhabited by the modern Kurds; as a consequence some Kurds claim the Guti as ancestors.

Erbil in the Ur III Period

Year names indicate that Erbil (Urbilum) was "destroyed" by Shulgi in his forty-fifth year and by Amar-Sin in his second year. However, as the city was evidently incorporated into the Ur III empire and integrated into the state administration it was probably besieged and taken rather than actually destroyed. It is not known whether or not the city had regained its independence from Gutian control prior to its incorporation with the Ur III empire. To date around a dozen texts from the Ur III admin-

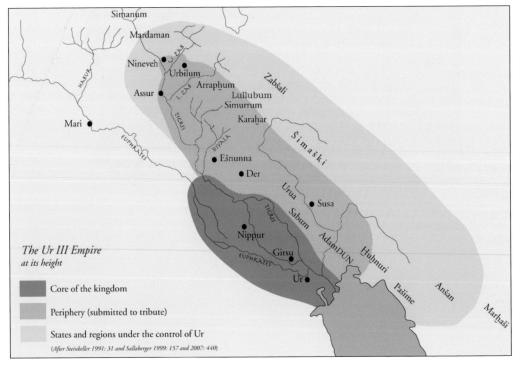

Map of the Ur III empire

istration mention Urbilum in one context or another. The taking of the city by Šulgi is reflected in transfer of the booty (*nam-ra-ak*) from Urbilum – silver, metal objects and sheep in year 45 and cattle in year 48. Cattle also appear as royal deliveries (mu-DU lugal) in Shulgi years 47 and 48, one consignment of which is further designated as tax (*maš-da-ri-a*) of the land of Urbilum. The city is likely to have remained part of the empire until almost the end. A votive inscription from Lagaš attests to the fact that it was still an integral province in the reign of Šu-Sin. In Šu-Sin year 7, 70 grass fed oxen are delivered as *gú ma-da* by the troops of Urbilum and a further delivery of oxen by the troops of Urbilum is recorded in Amar-Sin year 1. Logs were delivered to Urbilum from an institution called the *Eharhar*. Beer was issued to messengers to/from Urbilum and a number of individuals of Urbilum are recorded as the recipients of sheep, goats and oxen.

Erbil in the early second millennium

Erbil was a city within an independent state called Qabra (or Qabara) which was attacked by a coalition of Šamši-Adad I and Dadusha; it has been suggested that Erbil

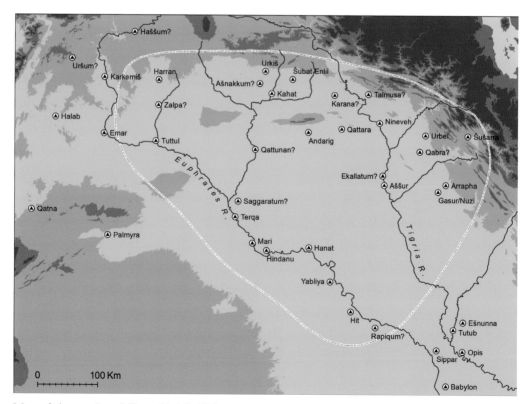

Map of the empire of Shamshi-Adad I (courtesy Jason Ur)

was the religious centre of this kingdom.[8] After the defeat and execution of Būnu-Ištar, Qabra passed into the control of Šamši-Adad I for some years following the campaign but he and his sons were not able to hold on to it when the Turukkean rebellion broke out. Note that the name of the city ruler is a name compounded with the goddess Ištar. This might be significant as it could be taken as evidence that Ištar was the tutelary goddess of Erbil in this period. Subsequent to the Turukkean rebellion Erbil must have become independent and remained so until its absorption into the Mittanni empire, probably in the late fifteenth century BC, though nothing is known about this in detail.

Erbil in the Middle Assyrian Period

Erbil (Arbail) was a major city in the late second millennium and must have formed part of the Middle Assyrian state for the majority of its existence. However control was evidently lost at some stage as in the course of his war with the Babylonian king Ninurta-nadin-šumi, the Assyrian king Aššur-rēša-iši (1133–1115 BC) had to march on Arbail.[9] The temple of Ištar was certainly already in existence: it was rebuilt by

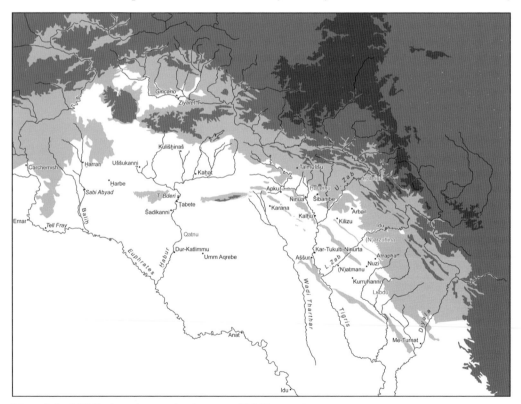

Map of the Middle Assyrian empire (courtesy J.N. Postgate)

8.   Charpin & Ziegler 2003 p. 92 n.136.

Shalmaneser I (1273–1244 BC), from whom we have the first attestation of its name, Egašankalamma, and the fact that it had a ziggurrat. Ištar received sheep from the palace and the king Enlil-kudurri-uṣur (1182–1179 BC) ordered her cultic clothing to be repaired. One Šamši-bel, a scribe of Arbail, dedicated a bronze statue there for the life of king Ashur-dan (I). The existence of a literary tradition is witnessed by the copying of omens. There was a palace in the city with an overseer (*rab ekalli*). Weapons were delivered to the palace and either the palace or the temple may have been decorated with glazed bricks. Though not yet directly attested, Arbail is certain to have been the seat of a provincial governor while the city itself also had a mayor (*ḥaziānu*). Regular offerings were sent from Arbail to the temple of Aššur in Assur as part of the *ginā'u* system of contributions from the provinces: these comprised barley, honey, sesame and fruit. Manpower was also supplied: millers to the Aššur temple and in the time of Tukulti-Ninurta I (13th century BC) deportees to work on the lower palace in Kar-Tukulti-Ninurta. The centralised control of labour is also evidence by the operation of an *iškāru* system of work quotas. Day to day business is evidenced by records concerning sheep, goats, grain, clothing and copper.

Erbil in the Neo-Assyrian period

In the Neo-Assyrian period Arbail ranked alongside Assur, Nineveh, Nimrud, Khorsabad and Kilizu as one of the most important cities of the Assyrian heartland. Its control over the wide fertile plains to the west ensured its flourishing prosperity while its location on the edge of the Zagros mountains made it both a nodal point in trade

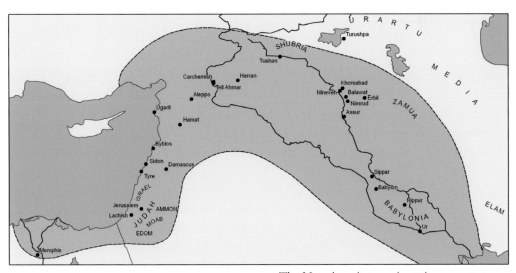

The Neo-Assyrian empire at its greatest extent

9.   cf. Brinkman 1968 p. 33, p. 99 n.538, p. 111 n.607, p. 314; this may have been due to Elamite incursions (Tenu 2009 p. 260).

with Iran and a centre of vital strategic importance. It has indeed been suggested that for Ashurbanipal the city served as a virtual second capital, and that he regularly sojourned here, particularly in the middle part of his reign.[10] Arbail was certainly home to a major military establishment and served as a natural point of departure and return for military campaigns in the northeast. This is directly attested for the reigns of Ashur-dan II, Ashurnasirpal II, Shalmaneser III and Ashurbanipal. The city was also host to celebrations on return from these campaigns. Such celebrations regularly included the torture and execution of captured opponents: Ashur-dan flayed alive Kundibhalle king of Katmuhu and draped his skin over the wall; Ashurnasirpal did exactly the same thing to Bubu king of Ništun and Ashurbanipal boasts of a whole string host of atrocities inflicted upon foreign leaders and emissaries.

There is particularly good documentation for the role played by Arbail in the sequence of events surrounding Ashurbanipal's campaigns against Teuman of Elam and Dunanu of Gambulu, as it is not only recorded in the annals of Ashurbanipal and associated inscriptions but also in two series of reliefs from Nineveh – the series in Room 23 of the Southwest Palace carved in around 650 BC and that in Room I of the North Palace carved in around 645 BC. Furthermore the associated epigraphs are preserved not just on the reliefs themselves but also on at least nine cuneiform tablets. In summary, Ashurbanipal was in Arbail when he was brought news of the insolent messages of Teuman, king of Elam. He prayed to Ištar and having being reassured by her launched his campaign, the targets of which were both Teuman and Dunanu the sheikh of the Gambulu. Following the successful completion of this campaign, Ashurbanipal returned to Nineveh and then progressed in triumph from Nineveh to Arbail (and then on to Assur).[11] Having arrived in Arbail, Ashurbanipal went out to the *akītu* house in the countryside at Milkia, made sumptuous offerings to Šatru and performed the *akītu* festival. At that time Dunanu was bound hand and foot in iron chains and brought to him. Ashurbanipal then made a triumphal entry into Arbail accompanied by Dunanu, Samgunu and Aplaya and the severed head of Teuman. He had Dunanu, Samgunu and Aplaya chained to a bear in the western and eastern gates of the city. He ripped out the tongues and flayed the skin of Mannu-ki-ahhē the deputy of Dunanu and Nabû-uṣalli, the prefect of the city of Gambulu.

Arbail city will certainly have had a substantial arsenal and chariots, horses, shields and bows are all variously mentioned in the sources. In a letter from the time of Sargon the author Aššur-alik-pani commits to bring his infantry, cavalry and chariotry to meet the king in the city. The city also served as a point of arrival for ambassadors coming from foreign lands (for example, Urartu and Elam) and also as the location

10. Villard 1995.

11. Weissert 1997, p. 350.

where city rulers from western Iran might deliver their tribute. In his Hymn to Arbail Ashurbanipal indeed proclaims "Tribute enters into it from all the world!". High ranking Assyrians and their messengers were received in Arbail. All these dignitaries and their emissaries might be issued with gold and silver rings and purple clothes.

Very little is known of the internal politics of Arbail. It was among the 27 cities which joined the rebellion of Aššur-danin-apli against Shalmaneser III and which were brought under submission by Šamši-Adad V. Occasionally letters in the royal correspondence report or hint at extortion and abuse. As regards building work, the major evidence is for work on the temples of Ištar in both Arbail and Milkia (see below), in addition to which Sennacherib organised the supply of water to Arbail by harnessing sources in the Hani mountains north of Arbail and constructing a *karez* system for bringing their water to the city. Following the conquest of Shubria, Esarhaddon gave captives to the temple of Ištar in Arbail along with the other major temples of Assyria and he also gave captives from Shubria to the citizens of Nineveh, Calah, Kilizu and Arbail. Arbail was likely home to a thriving mercantile community, although is not greatly represented in the texts other than in loans of silver and copper.

Arbail was the seat of a governor, who was in charge of the administration of the province and the organisation of the military; on four occasions the governor of Arbail served as eponym (787, 784, 759, 702 BC). The governor resided in the governor's palace, where payments of tax could be received and processed. Receipt was taken of payments of *ilku* (state labour contributions) including grapes, juniper, aromatics, *titipu* (a fruit), copper, leeks, pomegranates, grain, cakes and pistachios. Other important commodities were cattle, sheep and cloth. Administration of this system will have required the maintenance of up to date records of the province's population, their landholdings and obligations and census registers were compiled for this purpose. The city or province of Arbail was required to send offerings of sheep, wine, barley, emmer, oil, flour, honey, pomegranates and apples to the temple of Aššur in Assur. There may also have been a royal palace separate from governor's palace: note the proposal that in the latter years of his reign Ashurbanipal may indeed have used Arbail as his principal residence.[12]

There were weavers associated with the palace or temple (or both) responsible for the delivery of quotas of textiles (designated *iškāru*) and royal robes are mentioned occasionally in the official correspondence. It may be that the queen had a separate palace with her own staff in Arbail; other senior officials included the prefect (*šakin māti*), the steward (*masennu*) and the mayor (*ḫazānu*); each of these will also have had

12. Villard 1995 pp. 104–107.

their deputy. Court cases could be heard in Arbail. One verdict involves textiles and a yoke of oxen, other cases deal with the sale of slaves, ownership and sale of houses, fields and vineyards, the division of inheritances, business ventures, marriages and the redemption of a woman given as a pledge.

Ištar of Arbail

Ištar of Arbail was one of the highest gods of the Assyrian empire.[13] Starting at least with Sennacherib, and throughout the inscriptions of Esarhaddon and Ashurbanipal, Ištar of Arbail is regularly listed among the deities supporting the kings in their campaigns. Her involvement in military matters is also evident in a promise quoted by Ashurbanipal that she would bring about the downfall of Ahšeri the king of the Manneans, in the night vision sent by the goddess to Ashurbanipal's troops giving them confidence to cross the river Idide, and in her raining fire down upon the Arabs.

In legal texts Ištar of Arbail is mentioned as one of the deities by which the parties swear and who will administer punishment upon any contravenor. A typical example is that "any future litigator is to pay 5 minas of silver and 1 mina of gold to Ištar of Arbail and to return the money tenfold to its owners"; there are many variations on the exact amounts of the gold and the silver stipulated. Other curses call upon Ištar to afflict the culprit with leprosy and to deny access to temple and palace. Ištar of Arbail is similarly invoked in the formula of curses against anyone who destroys literary tablets. Along with other gods Ištar of Arbail also appears in the greetings formulae of letters to the king from Assyrian scholars.

Ištar's temple in Arbail was called the Egašankalamma – the "House of the Lady of the Land". In the Neo-Assyrian period it is first referred to by Shalmaneser III. As far as we know it was next the object of extensive rebuilding and renovation on the part of Esarhaddon, for which the greatest detail is given in a cylinder from Nimrud: "He clothed Egašankalamma, the temple of Ištar of Arbail, his lady, with *zahalû*[14] and made it shine like the day. He had fashioned lions, lion-headed eagles, bulls and naked heroes and griffins of silver and gold and set them up in the entrance of its gates". Ashurbanipal also records that he rebuilt the residence of Ištar of Arbail and clothed its walls in silver and gold. The standards which he boasts of renovating may be those depicted in the Louvre relief flanking the uppermost entrance to the temple.

13. An earlier review of the evidence for the cult in Arbail can be found in Menzel 1981 pp. 6–11.

14. As in one source Esarhaddon says that he covered the Egašankalamma with silver and gold and in the other source with *zahalû*, in both cases using the phrase "so that it shone like day", we may be justified in concluding that in this case *zahalû* means an alloy of silver and gold (electrum).

Cylinder seal depicting a eunuch worshipping the cult statue of Ishtar of Arbail
(British Museum, London – BM 89769)

As regards the appearance of the cult image, according to both the description in the dream of Ashurbanipal's seer and the depiction on the stele from Til Barsip Ištar was represented standing on a lion with a sword and quiver hanging either side (the only difference is that in the stele the sword is sheathed whereas in the dream it is drawn ready for battle).[15] In Ashurbanipal's Hymn to Arbail, Ištar is "seated on a lion .... mighty lions crouch below her, kings of (all) land(s) are cowered before her, [she holds] domination over beasts". The goddess wore a headdress topped by a star and may have carried an aegis symbolising the protective radiance (*melammu*) with which she was imbued. She may have been surrounded by fire: a flame burst forth at the end of the Ashurbanipal's seer's night vision and when Ištar of Arbail assists the same king against the Arabs she is described as clothed in fire and bearing a *melammu*. The main cult statue was flanked by images of the king and a massive offering table stood in front of it.

There was a high decree of syncretism with other female deities: Ištar of Arbail was closely identified with Mullissu (Ninlil) and must have also been perceived as having close connections with Ištar of Nineveh and the Assyrian Ištar. In the cult centre of Milkia, outside Arbail, Ištar of Arbail was known as Šatru (see below). Very little is known about cultic procedure. Offerings certainly included sheep, wine and beer but will in reality have been much more extensive that that. Evidently there were rituals which mirrored or recreated events on/of the supernatural level. References in letters to the *taklimtu* – the exposing of the body of the dead – probably refer to rites

15. The quivers hanging either side of Ištar are also mentioned in a fragmentary section of the Nergal-Laṣ inscription (K 2631+): Borger 1996 p. 84 l.50.

of Dumuzi. A letter written after Esarhaddon's triumphal entry into Arbail in 670 BC reports that rituals were carried out against possible cultic offences.

Music clearly played an important part in the cult. Shalmaneser III marked his restoration of the temple harp (*tibu'* = *timbuttu*) with the composition of a hymn in which he makes clear it was an exceptional object embellished with copper and gold and crowned with a star of amber. Possibly the harp was restored and the hymn composed as part of the victory celebrations held in Arbail at the conclusion of Shalmaneser's campaign against Urartu; at any rate the verse account certainly appears to have been composed for this occasion. It is similarly likely that Ashurbanipal's Hymn to Arbail was composed for his triumphal entry into the city, and we must expect that Esarhaddon will also have commissioned such compositions for his triumphal entries into Arbail although to date these have not been recovered. Ashurbanipal's Hymn to Arbail mentions a number of further instruments: the lyre (*pilaggu*), *pigû* drum, *dubdubbu* drum and kettledrums (*lilissu*). Cultic performers including *kurgarrû* (cultic performers) and *kalû* (lamentation priests) are also likely to have been involved.

Arbail was the seat of ecstatic phrophetesses who uttered oracular pronouncements. Most attestations are from the time of Esarhaddon and Ashurbanipal. The pronouncements concern the safety of the king (including that his food and drink will not be poisoned), the assurance that he will live a long life, the succession of his offspring, the searching out of traitors and bringing order to the land, the defeat of the king's enemies, appointment of governors, and the choice of emissaries to send to foreign rulers. Pronouncements on some of these issues might also be made to the Queen Mother and the utterances might be reported to the king in the governor's correspondence. Extispiscies before Šamaš and Adad were also performed on these matters in Arbail with the reports quoting the relevant apodoses from omen collections. From Ashurbanipal's Hymn to Arbail we know that Nanāya and Sin were also worshipped in Arbail and there will certainly have been many other temples and shrines. Together with Ištar of Nineveh, Ištar of Arbail held a special place with the Assyrian royal family and it may be that at least some of the royal children spent their childhood in the temples of Ištar in Nineveh and Arbail; this is probably what is meant by Ashurbanipal's statement in his Hymn to the Ištars of Nineveh and Arbail "I knew no father or mother, I grew up in the lap of my goddesses".

Religious activities were only one part of the life of the temple of Ištar, which was also deeply involved in day to day business of a secular nature. Firstly the Egašankalamma will have owned extensive estates, the tending of which will have required a large force of farmers, gardeners and shepherds together with all the staff required for their administration. Senior officials included the chief administrator (*šangû*) and a steward (*laḫḫinu*). The temple will also have had a full complement of artisans – smiths, carpenters, leatherworkers, textile workers, potters, jewellers – producing materials for the temple's own use, for supply to the state and for sale. Finally, the temple acted in the capacity of a bank, lending out silver, copper and grain to merchants and other private individuals; this aspect is particularly well documented.

The staff of the temple included a large number of male and female oblates for which two terms, *kezru/kezretu* and *šēlūtu*, were used. The source of such individuals was partly voluntary dedications by their parents as owners and partly from individuals requisitioned through the legal system as a result of penalties stipulated in contracts. Oblates are likely to have been involved in all professions required by the temple – agricultural workers, food processors (butchers, bakers, brewers, cooks, oil pressers), artisans of all types, and those involved in the cult (singers, dancers, musicians, acrobats, sacrificial arrangers, *kulmašītu*'s, ecstatics, clergy). Oblates could marry and at least some of the servants/slaves (*urdu*) of Ištar might be exempted from state obligations.

The temple was also home to a scribal school. This is likely to have been one of the major schools of Assyria although direct evidence is limited: the King List from Khorsabad was written by a scribe of the temple of Arbail and one of the manuscripts of the Assyrian Royal Chronicle was written by a scribe of the temple (although it was actually written in Assur). From the reign of Esarhaddon or Ashurbanipal a number of letters are extant from foreman of the decury of scribes of Arbail to the crown prince: these concern astronomical observations such as eclipses and the meteorological conditions relevant to trying to observe the moon. Other texts record the distribution of meat to scholars (*ummânu*) of Arbail. A letter from the reign of Esarhaddon states that the scribes of Nineveh, Kilizu and Arbail could go ahead and enter a treaty ceremony (*adê*) although those of Assur had not yet come.

Milkia

Outside of the city Ištar had a second cult installation at Milkia, where there was a countryside *akītu* house, very likely identical with the Palace of the Steppe (Egaledinna).[16] Ištar was worshipped here in the form of Šatru. An *akītu* ceremony will have been carried out here once or twice a year. Ištar will have travelled to Milkia for this in her chariot[17] and her journey and sojourn there were reported in the royal correspon-

---

16. For previous discussions of the cultic installation at Milkia see Menzel 1981 p. 113 and Pongratz-Leisten 1994 pp. 79–82.

17. Menzel 1981 p. 276 + n.3710.

dence. Milkia is also the subject of at least one oracular pronouncement. When the Assyrian kings carried out victory celebrations in Arbail, festivities at Milkia formed part of the programme. Thus Shalmaneser III, Esarhaddon and Ashurbanipal all record celebrating the festival (*isinnu*) of Šatru in Milkia. The principal meal in the programme at Milkia was the *qarītu*, an *al fresco* banquet whose menu included fruit, lamb, birds, *aṣudu* (soup), bread, honey, oil, wine and beer; there were directions for how to correctly set up the tables bearing these offerings.

Esarhaddon and Ashurbanipal both rebuilt or renovated the *akītu* house in Milkia and it is not unlikely that Shalmaneser III will have done the same. Esarhaddon gives the most detailed description:

> [I ...] the *akītu* house in the open countryside, the house of merry making, and restored its rites. [I renovated] that [temple] with baked bricks, haematite and lapis lazuli and built it with lofty cedar beams and [...] its [...]. On the seventeenth day of Ululu I [...] hastened to bring their offerings before them. With deep insight and profound wisdom I settled them in the *akītu* house. [....], 10 sheep, 10 birds, 7 homers of wine, 4 homers of [...], groats beer (*ḫašlatu*), [all] this I established before them for the table of their divinities in the *akītu* house in the open countryside.

Evidently Sargon also carried out work in Milkia as this is referred to in letters to the king.[18]

Erbil in the Neo-Babylonian and Achaemenid Periods

With the partition of the Assyrian empire following the fall of Nineveh Erbil probably fell to the share of the Medes, component ancestors of the modern Kurds.[19] The statuette of Šamši-bel was probably looted from the Egašankalamma at this time and was found near Lake Urmia, in what was probably Median territory. At some stage Erbil may or may not have subsequently passed into Babylonian control. Either way it was certainly then incorporated into the Achaemenid empire. It is disappointing that so little material has been recovered relating to Erbil in these times.

In the inscription of Behistun Darius records hunting down and impaling the rebel Shitrantakhma in Erbil. The importance of the city as a provincial centre in the Ach-

---

18. Perhaps the dais (*parakku*) of Ištar of Arbail mentioned in a field sale refers to the installation at Milkia.

19. See Curtis 2003 pp. 166–167.

Medes as depicted in the Persepolis reliefs.

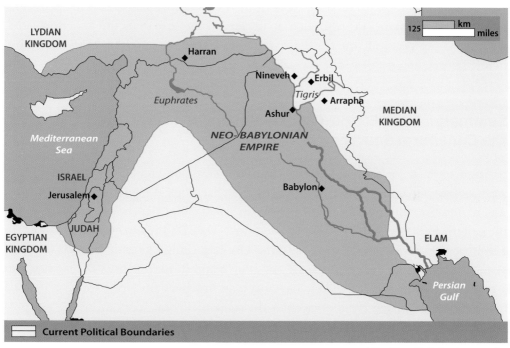

The Neo-Babylonian empire

aemenid Empire is attested both by the passport of Nehtihur and by references in the classical sources, while an administrative text from the Ebabbara temple in Sippar indicates that by the time of Cyrus normal exchange between Erbil and southern Mesopotamia had resumed. Unpublished texts in Elamite from Persepolis may one day shed light on the role of the city within the Achaemenid imperial administration. One final piece of evidence comes from a Babylonian astronomical diary which,

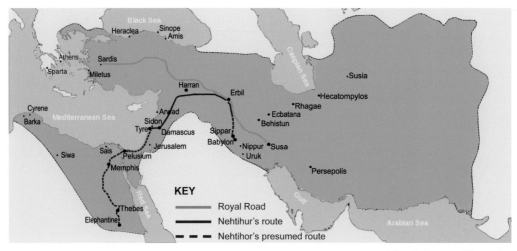

The Achaemenid empire

amongst other things, preserves details from Alexander's final battle with Darius up to his entry into Babylon. Although as preserved the text does not mention Erbil, we know from classical sources that Alexander stayed there briefly after his victory before proceeding south to the capital.

Summary: from Erridu-Pizir to Alexander – Erbil in the Cuneiform Sources

Situated on a major trade route into Iran and commanding the rich plains to the west, Erbil was destined to be a great city. Archaeological evidence indicates there was a presence here by the Ubaid period (*ca.* 5500–4000 BC) but it is possible that the origins may stretch back beyond even that. There is no further information for Erbil for that period, nor for the ensuing Uruk or Early Dynastic periods, but it is virtually certain that in the course of the fourth and third millennia BC it grew into a major city which will very likely have been an independent city state with its own native dynasties. When Erbil does enter the stage of history, conditions are not propitious. Apart from references to messengers going to Erbil in texts from Ebla, the first really historical information on the city is in an inscription of Erridu-Pizir, a king of the Guti who lived some time around 2200 BC, who records conquering the city and capturing its governor Nirišhuha. It is not known whether Erbil regained its independence when the Gutians were expelled from Mesopotamia by Utu-hegal and Ur-Nammu – it is conceivable that it may, at least initially, have stayed under Gutian control – but it was in any case certainly a target of military campaigns half a century later. In his forty-fifth year "Shulgi the strong man, the king of Ur, the king of the four quarters, smashed the heads of Urbilum, Simurrum, Lullubum and Karhar in

a single campaign". The city was incorporated into the Ur III empire and administrative texts document the delivery of booty and taxes in the form of cattle, sheep, silver and bronze. Evidently however the hold on the region was not unbreakable as five years later Amar-Sin had to return and "destroy" the city again.

Nothing is known about Erbil during the remaining part of the Ur III empire other than that it remained part of the provincial network. At some stage around 2000 BC Ur lost control of the region, at which point Erbil may have regained its independence but then came to be included in the kingdom of Qabra. When (around 1716 BC) Dadusha of Eshnunna and Shamshi-Adad I formed their coalition to campaign in northeastern Mesopotamia, Qabra was invaded and Erbil taken. There are extant stelae of each of these kings documenting these events. For some years following the campaign Qabra passed into the control of Šamši-Adad but he and his sons were not able to hold on to the region when the Turukkean rebellion broke out; there is in any case no further information on Erbil during the time of Šamši-Adad's occupation. Once again the city appears to have re-

Foundation figurine of king Shulgi of Ur, carrying a basket (Metropolitan Museum, New York – 59.41.1).

gained its autonomy and probably remained independent until its absorption into the Mittanni empire, about which nothing is known in detail, and which in turn came to an end with the rise of the Middle Assyrian empire in the fourteenth century BC. By the reign of Shalmaneser I (1273–1244 BC) at the latest Erbil had come to be included within the core territory of Assyria, a situation which then essentially lasted till the end of the Assyrian empire in 612 BC although there may have been occasions, for example during the reign of Aššur-rēša-iši (1133–1115 BC), when this control was lost. With the Middle Assyrian period the variety of evidence available increases somewhat and we begin to get a glimpse of the affairs of the city, now a provincial capital and home to both a governor and a mayor. The palace was involved in the collection of taxes and also trade. Particularly well attested are the regular offerings comprising barley, honey, sesame and fruit sent from Erbil to the temple of Aššur in Assur as part of the *ginā'u* system of provincial contributions. Obligations to supply manpower are also evident in millers sent to the temple of Aššur and in deportees sent to work on the construction of Kar-Tukulti-Ninurta.

With the Neo-Assyrian period the sources for Erbil really come into their own. There are over 200 occurrences in the cuneiform texts, including official inscriptions of seven different kings, royal correspondence, administrative texts, hymns, reports on oracles and divination, a votive inscription and a cultic commentary. The city functioned as an important military stronghold and served as a natural point of departure for military campaigns in the northeast and as the scene of celebrations at their conclusion. Triumphal entries into the city are attested for Esarhaddon after his conquest of Egypt in 670 BC and for Ashurbanipal after his conquest of Elam in 653 BC. Ashurbanipal's campaigns against Teuman and Dunanu are also depicted in series of sculptures from both the Southwest Palace and the North Palace in Nineveh. The military administration came under the governor who was also responsible for the receipt of tribute and the collection of taxes. The city was also the regional centre for the administration of justice. The city or province of Arbail was itself required to send offerings of sheep, wine, barley, emmer, oil, flour, honey, pomegranates and apples to the temple of Aššur in Assur. The well being of Erbil itself was served when in the early seventh century Sennacherib constructed a canal to bring water to the city

With the carving up of the Assyrian empire after the fall of Nineveh Erbil almost certainly fell into the control of the Medes. It is not known whether at any stage it subsequently passed into the control of the Neo-Babylonian empire, but there is no evidence that it did. There is no information at all on Erbil itself during this time. Following Cyrus' invasion of Babylonia in 539 BC the city was however certainly incorporated within the Achaemenid empire and it was in Erbil that Darius I had the rebel Shitrantakhma impaled. Under the Achaemenids the city must have been a flourishing provincial capital though the only direct evidence for this is its occurrence in the itinerary in the Passport of Nehtihor.

Ištar of Arbail

Ištar of Arbail was one of the highest gods of the Assyrian empire. Alongside Aššur, Sin, Šamaš, Marduk, Nabû, Ištar of Nineveh and others she is regularly invoked by Assyrian kings as one of the principal gods supporting their campaigns. She also features in the greetings formulae of letters in the royal correspondence and among the deities by whom treaties are sworn.

The cult image represented Ištar standing on a lion, holding a sword, quivers hanging either side, and wearing a headdress topped by a star. The image may have been surrounded by fire and Ištar's protective radiance (*melammu*) may have been represented in some way. The image will have had an extensive and elaborate wardrobe but little is known of this. Only fragments are known about details of the cult: in the Middle Assyrian period there was a ceremony called the *nugatīpu* of Ištar, while in the Neo-

Assyrian period the principal festival (*isinnu*) appears to have been the *akītu* at Milkia. Music clearly played an important part in ceremonies. Shalmaneser III restored the temple harp, decorating it with mountain animals and crowning it with a star of amber, celebrating this event in a hymn composed for the occasion. Other types of lyres and drums are also known. The personnel required for the cult will have included singers, dancers, musicians, acrobats, sacrificial arrangers, *kulmašītu*'s, ecstatics, *kalû*'s (lamentation priests) and other clergy. Hundreds of votive offerings must have been made to Ištar in Arbail but to date only one – the statuette of Shamshi-bel – has been recovered and even this had been taken away as booty in antiquity. There is however also a votive stele to Ištar of Arbail with a depiction of the goddess from Til Barsip.

Egašankalamma

Ištar's main temple in Arbail was known as the Egašankalamma. Its origins are likely to lie far back in time, by analogy with other temples in Mesopotamia perhaps as far back as the Ubaid period. Ištar's connection with the city is perhaps hinted at by the fact that Būnu-Ištar, the ruler defeated by Dadusha and Šamši-Adad I, bore a name compounded with the name of the goddess. The actual temple is however not directly attested until the time of Shalmaneser I (1273–1244 BC), who records that he "built the Egašankalamma, the temple of Ištar the Lady of Arbail, my lady, together with its ziggurrat". By the late Assyrian period it was clearly a major complex. It was the subject of extensive renovations on the part of Esarhaddon: "He

clothed Egašankalamma, the temple of Ištar of Arbail, his lady, with gold alloy [20] and made it shine like the day. He had fashioned lions, lion-headed *anzû*-birds, bulls, naked heroes and griffins of silver and gold and set them up in the entrance of its gates". Esarhaddon's rebuilding of the temple of Ištar was probably undertaken from spoils taken from Egypt. Further work was done by Ashurbanipal, who also restored the temple standards. Ashurbanipal had hymns composed to Arbail and to the Ištars of Arbail and Nineveh and it is probable that both the rebuildings and the

The model of a reconstruction of the Esagila temple in Babylon in the Pergamon Museum, Berlin, gives an impression of an Assyrian temple. The relief of Arbail in the Louvre shows a temple façade of a similar style rising above the walls of the Citadel.

20. As in one source Esarhaddon says that he covered the Egašankalama with silver and gold and in the other source with *zaḫalû*, in both cases using the phrase "so that it shone like day", we may be justified in concluding that in this case *zaḫalû* means an alloy of silver and gold (electrum).

composition of the hymns comprised part of the victory celebrations following the campaign against Teuman and Dunanu. Shalmaneser III's hymn to Ištar of Arbail recording the restoration of the temple harp was likewise probably composed to mark the celebrations of one of his campaigns in the northeast, perhaps the campaign against Urartu of his third year. Accordingly it is not unlikely that Esarhaddon will also have commissioned a hymn as part of his celebrations following the conquest of Egypt but this has not yet been recovered.

The temple of Ištar was the seat of ecstatic phrophetesses who uttered oracular pronouncements. These mostly date to the reigns of Esarhaddon and Ashurbanipal and chiefly concern the safety of the king, the defeat of his enemies and the stability of the land. Together with Ištar of Nineveh, Ištar of Arbail was particularly responsible for the wellbeing of the king and his family and it may be that at least some of the royal children spent their childhood in the temples of Ištar in Nineveh and Arbail.

The temple will certainly have had a sumptuous schedule of offerings but to date only sheep, wine and beer are directly attested. According to a decree of either Esarhaddon or Ashurbanipal, the obligation to supply some of these offerings may have been placed upon estates in Raṣappa, Bit-Zamani and Uppumu, provinces far distant from Arbail. The temple will also have had its own extensive landholdings, both in the province of Arbail and other parts of the empire. The administration of these estates will have required a large force of farmers, shepherds, orchard keepers and birdtenders, together with an extensive bureaucracy. At the top of this administration was the *šangû* of the Egašankalamma. There will have been a scribal school, where scribes were trained, literary texts copied, and which very likely provided the core of scholars required for astronomical observations. The Egašankalamma certainly had a staff of bakers, brewers, cooks and gardeners and will also have employed a large body of artisans (smiths, carpenters, leatherworkers, textile workers, potters, jewellers and others) as well as those involved in the cult listed above. Many of these individuals will have been oblates dedicated to the temple for which two terms, *šelūtu* and *kezru*, are used. One source of these oblates was free will offerings but others may also have entered the temple in fulfillment of penalty obligations stipulated in legal contracts. At least some of the servants/slaves (*urdu*) of Ištar might be exempted from state obligations.

The Egašankalamma will have had a treasury for the safekeeping of temple funds and treasures. Major sources of income will have been revenue from temple fields and property, from the sale of agricultural produce and manufactured goods and from private donations. The payment of gold and silver to Ištar of Arbail was a penalty clause frequently stipulated in legal contracts so perhaps this too was a source of some income. The temple in turn acted in the capacity of a bank, lending out silver, copper and grain to merchants and other individuals

Milkia

Ištar's second cult installation was the *akītu* house called the Palace of the Steppe (Egaledinna) in the countryside outside of the city at Milkia. She traveled here in her chariot and was worshipped in the form of Šatru. Milkia is first attested in the reign of Shalmaneser III. It is not unlikely that this king will have restored the temple there, and we know that some work was carried out in the reign of Sargon, but it is only with Esarhaddon and Ashurbanipal that we have any descriptions. Shalmaneser III, Esarhaddon and Ashurbanipal all record celebrating the festival (*isinnu*) of Šatru in Milkia. The principal meal in the festival programme was the *qarītu*, an outdoor banquet whose menu included fruit, lamb, birds, soup, bread, honey, oil, wine and beer; there were directions for how to correctly set up the tables bearing these offerings.

Conclusion

In conclusion, Erbil is attested in cuneiform texts from the late third millennium up until the mid first millennium BC. Over this period the writing of the city's name in cuneiform texts progresses from Irbilum (Ebla) to Urbilum (Ur III) to Urbēl (early second millennium) to Arbail (Middle and Neo-Assyrian periods). The first really historical attestation records the city being sacked by Erridu-Pizir, in the Ur III period it was sacked by Shulgi and subsequently retaken by Amar-Sin, and then taken again in the second millennium by Shamshi-Adad I and Dadusha. From the Middle Assyrian period Erbil became the seat of a provincial government with palace and governor, the latter responsible for the reception of foreign dignitaries, receipt of tribute, collection of taxes, the sending of contributions to the temple of Aššur in Assur and command of the military establishment. The city was a springboard for military campaigns and the scene of celebrations upon their conclusion. On the civil side Erbil benefited from the construction by Sennacherib of a canal bringing water to the city.

Ištar of Arbail was one of the supreme deities of Assyria. Her primary temple was the Egašankalamma, directly attested first in the time of Shalmaneser I, who renovated both the temple and its ziggurrat, but with roots which will have stretched far back beyond that. The Egašankalamma was the subject of lavish attention on the part of Esarhaddon and Ashurbanipal. The temple will have had extensive estates and a large staff but little is known of the cult. The temple was home to ecstatics who made oracular pronouncements. Ištar's other shrine was the Egaledinna in the countryside at Milkia where she was worshipped in the form of Šatru in an *akītu* festival and in victory ceremonies.

This brings an end to our survey of the Erbil as an ancient Mesopotamian city. When Alexander the Great pitted himself against Darius III the decisive battle Guagamela was fought in the plains northwest of Erbil. This marked the transition into a new phase of civilization and forms a fitting end to our account of Erbil in the cuneiform sources.

The Sources

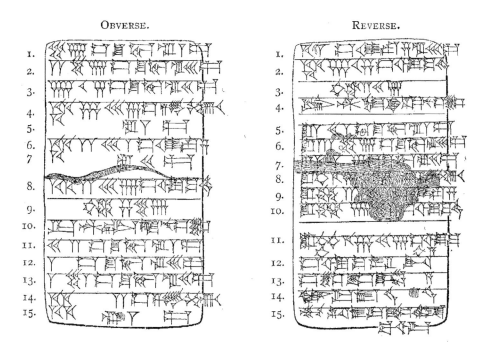

Third Millennium Sources

Ebla Texts

Three documents from the archives of the palace of Ebla in northwestern Syria may mention Erbil. Two topographs come into consideration – *Ir-bí-ì-lum*[ki] (attested twice) and *ù-ra*-BÍL[ki] (attested once). It is not certain that these spellings both refer to the same toponym but it does seem likely that *Ir-bí-ì-lum*[ki] really does refer to Erbil. The first two of these documents deal with the issuing of silver for a messenger going to Erbil and date to the viziership of Ibbi-zikir, around 2300–2280 BC by the middle chronology. This was a time when the geographic horizons of Ebla reached far and wide, including contacts with Assur and Gasur. In the case of the third document, which deals with textiles, the identification with Erbil is much less secure: the ending -*um* is missing, the use of *ù*- is unexpected and an identification with the Syrian toponym *ù-ra-bal*[ki] seems equally if not in fact more probable.

TM.75.G.2428 obv.xxiv.3   (MEE 1, 1867)[21]
A very long list of annual disbursements of metals including the issue of "five shekels of silver as provisions for the journey of Tilani, one of the messengers who is going to Erbil (*Ir-bí-ì-lum*[ki])". Dated to year 8 of Ibbi-zikir the vizier under king Ishar-damu.

TM.75.G.2429 obv.xiii.26   (MEE 12, 36)[22]
A very long text listing annual disbursements of metals including the issue of "five shekels of silver as provisions for the journey of Tilani, one of the messengers who is going to Erbil (*Ir-bí-ì-lum*[ki])". Dated to year 10 of Ibbi-zikir the vizier under king Ishar-damu.

ARET I 31.obv.ii.3
This text contains a reference to "one *guzitum*-cloth – Darmash of Urabil". The toponym is written *ù-ra*-BÍL[ki]. The same individual Darmash appears in another text concerning cloth from a place Nirar or Irar (NI-*ra-ar*[ki]) which is thought to be have been near Ebla to the north.

21.   Pettinato 1979 No. 1867, Astour 1987 p. 11, Waetzoldt 2001 p. 263f No. 35.

22.   Pettinato 1979 No. 1868, Matthiae 1977 plate at back, Astour 1987 p. 11, Waetzoldt 2001 p. 407f No. 36.

Gutian Sources

Erbil next enters history in an inscription of Erridu-pizir, a king of Gutium who probably ruled in the interval between the end of the Akkadian empire and the foundation of the Ur III state; a more exact placing of this king cannot be given at present. Nor can a date be given for his reign more accurate than 2200 BC ± 100 years. Gutium was the designation for a people who by the Old Babylonian period were seated in the mountainous region northeast of the lower Tigris, but who in the third millennium may have been localised in the mid-Euphrates area and/or northern Babylonia.[23] In the late third millennium the Gutians were seen by the mainstream Mesopotamian states as a constant threat, and they did indeed bring about the end of the Akkadian empire.

Erridu-Pizir

RIME II Erridu-pizir E2.2.1.3
(p. 227)[24]

Inscription of the Gutian king Erridu-pizir in which he describes himself as "the mighty one, king of Gutium, king of the four quarters" and briefly summarises his campaign against Simirrum, Lullubum and Urbilum. This inscription was originally composed for a statue of Erridu-Pizir but is only known from an Old Babylonian tablet which gives copies of the inscriptions on three statues of the king. The passage relevant to our purposes reads as follows (xi.1–11):

> In a single day he brought ... down and conquered the pass of Urbilum at Mount Murnum. Further he (captured) Nirišhuha, the gover[nor] of Urbi[lum]

Hecht Museum, Haifa

23. Hallo RlA Band 3 p. 719 "Gutium".

24. Frayne 1993.

Based on this inscription Kutscher concludes that the city of Urbilum lay in the territory of Lullubum,[25] but this would seem to be contradicted by sources which list the two names together in a manner suggesting they are different places. Furthermore in this very inscription Kanišba is given as the king (*lugal*) of Simirrum while Niriḫuha is the ruler (*ensi*) of Urbilum (there is no necessary implication that an *ensi* was dependent on a *lugal*). As also noted by Kutscher,[26] the name of the ruler Niriḫuha is Hurrian and this may be taken as evidence that the population of Urbilum at that time was Hurrian or at least included a Hurrian component.

Ur III Sources

The period of Gutian domination came to an end with the reestablishment of Sumerian control over Mesopotamia. The first steps were taken by Utu-hegal when he expelled the Gutians from the land. His period of dominance was however short lived as he was in his turn ousted by one of his own officials, Ur-Nammu, who thereby initiated the Third Dynasty of Ur and went on to create the Neo-Sumerian empire. Sources for Erbil (Urbilum) in this period include year names attesting to the destruction of the city, a votive inscription and a number of references in administrative documents.

Year names

In the late third and early second millennium cuneiform texts were dates by a system of year names in which each year was named after a significant event that occurred in that year. Two such year names are relevant to the history of Erbil:[27]

25. Kutscher 1989 p. 69.

26. Kutscher 1989 p. 70.

27. For references see (1) http://cdli.ucla.edu/tools/yearnames, (2) http://bdtns.filol.csic.es.

Year name for Shulgi year 45

mu ^{d}šul-gi nita kalag-ga lugal uri${}_{2}{}^{ki}$-ma lugal an ub-da limmu${}_{2}$-ba-ke${}_{4}$ ur-bi${}_{2}$-lum^{ki} si-mu-ru-um^{ki} lu-lu-bu^{ki} ù ka-ra${}_{2}$-har^{ki} 1-šè aš-šè sag-du-bi šu-bur${}_{2}$-a bi${}_{2}$-ra-a im-mi-ra

Year in which Shulgi the strong man, the king of Ur, the king of the four quarters, smashed the heads of Urbilum, Simurrum, Lullubum and Karhar in a single campaign

Diminutive clay tablet 3 cm square dated "the year Urbilum was destroyed"; it does not state whether this was by Shulgi or Amar-Sin (Bridwell Library, Dallas – Tablet 9, image courtesy of Bridwell Library Special Collections, Perkins School of Theology, Southern Methodist University).

Year name for Amar-Sin year 2

mu ^{d}amar-^{d}en.zu lugal-e ur-bi${}_{2}$-lum^{ki} mu-hul

Year Amar-Sin the king destroyed Urbilum

In some cases the king responsible is not specified and such tablets could be dated to either Shulgi year 45 or Amar-Sin year 2.

Clay tablet dated on the reverse "the year Amar-Sin destroyed Urbilum" (California Museum of Ancient, Los Angeles, 002-C0006).

Votive Inscription

RIME 3/2 Šū-Sîn E3/2.1.4.13 (p. 324)[28]

An inscription found on four door socket from Girsu, evidently from a temple dedicated to Šū-Sîn by Ir-Nanna. Ir-Nanna was chief vizier (*sukkalmah*) from late in the reign of Shulgi through to the disintegration of the Ur III empire under Ibbi-Sin;[29] in this inscription he claims to be governor of Urbilum among other places.

> For Šū-Sîn, beloved of the god Enlil, the king whom the god Enlil chose in his (own) heart, mighty king, king of Ur, king of the four quarters, his lord: Ir-Nanna grand-vizier, governor of Lagaš, sanga (priest) of the god Enki, governor of Ušar-Garšana, governor of Bašime, governor of Sabum and the land of Gutebum, governor of Di-mat-Enlila, governor of Āl-Šū-Sîn, governor of Urbilum, governor of Hamazi and Karahar, governor of NI.HI, governor of Šimaški and the land of Karda, his servant built for him his Girsu temple.

Administrative Texts

Texts from Girsu

SAT 1, 377	Šu-Sin 07	32 logs of ùr-ù-suh₅ and éš-dím delivered to Urbilum from É-HAR.HAR; from Nanmah; of the é-ᵈŠu-ᵈSuen; sealed by Abba, a messenger of the king
TCTI 2, 3899	Šu-Sin 07	issue of beer to messengers from Urbilum

Texts from Drehem

Trouvaille, 86	Šulgi 45	metal objects, booty (nam-ra-ak) of Urbilum
MVN 13, 423	Šulgi 45	sheep, booty (nam-ra-ak) of Urbilum, issued to individuals described as MAR.TU (Amorite)

---

28. Frayne 1997.

29. Potts 1994 p. 137.

AUCT 2 326+336	Šulgi 45?[30]	5½ shekels of silver (al-hul-a), booty (nam-ra-ak) of Urbilum delivered to and received within Puzriš-Dagan
PDT 2 1151	Šulgi 46	sheep and goats sent to the kitchen on behalf of a man of Urbilum (as well as some Amorites and a man from Hešumma)
BIN 3, 018	Šulgi 47	1 ox delivered by Sadazi, a man of Urbilum; part of a royal delivery (mu-DU lugal) which also includes 10 cattle designated as the maš-da-ri-a of the land of Urbilum
AUCT 2 384	Šulgi 47	man of Urbilum delivering metal objects; these items were delivered and received within Ur; tablet damaged
Ontario 1 053	Šulgi 48	3 oxen and 3 female calves, booty (nam-ra-ak) of Urbilum, royal delivery
CHEU 006	Šu-Sin 07	delivery of 70 grass fed oxen delivered as gú ma-da (a tax specific to the peripheral regions north and east of the core Ur III state) by the troops of Urbilum (the text also mentions deliveries of še-ti-ir-ša^{ki})[31]
MVN 11,180	Amar-Sin 01	6 oxen and 1 cow delivered by the troops of Urbilum (also deliveries from Amorites and the ensi of Nippur)
CT 32 26.18	Amar-Sin 07	5 sheep for the daughter in law (or bride) of Nanipatal of Urbilum[32]

30. As mentioned, if not further qualified "the year Urbilum was destroyed" can refer to either Šulgi 45 or Amar-Sin 02.

31. Steinkeller, 1987 p. 35 n. 48; Maeda 1992 p. 171.

32. A known official of Urbilum, Na-ni-ba/pá-tal, who also appears in CT 32 27, might be the same official who appears on TCL 2 5500, and on PDT 554. The tablet is illustrated on the following page.

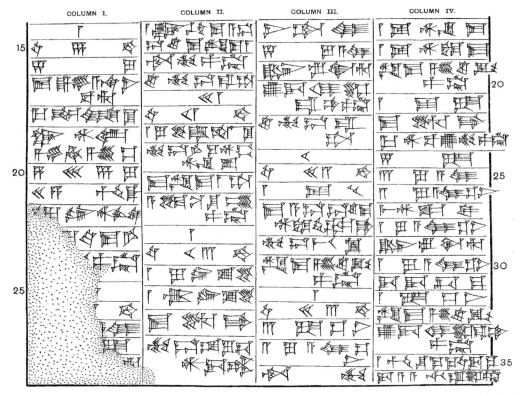

COLUMN I.   COLUMN II.   COLUMN III.   COLUMN IV.

CT 32 26.18 – British Museum, London (BM 103450)

MVN 13 726   [no date]   expenditure of normal beer (kaš-gen) for the messenger of Urbilum

In two further texts detailing the receipt of booty (AUCT 2 284, AUCT 1 28) Urbilum is not actually named but the fact that the texts date to Amar-Sin year 2, a year in which Urbilum was destroyed, makes it likely that the reference here are indeed to booty from Urbilum.

Early Second Millennium Sources

The fall of the Ur III state led to a major reconfiguration of the political geography of Mesopotamia. This is better documented for the south, where the successor states formed a patchwork of kingdoms across Babylonia until eventually unified by Hammurapi. In the north the city of Assur regained its independence, leading to the emergence of a nascent Assyrian state. Sources for Erbil in the early second millennium are scarce, in fact only two sources are known for this period, both stelae bearing royal inscriptions. One of these is fragmentary but may be attributed to Šamši-Adad I, the other is of Dadusha. Both stelae describe events of the same campaign in which these kings joined forces to invade the northeast of Mesopotamia.[33] As noted in the introduction, the chronology for this period is not fixed, but following a shorter chronology these events may be dated to approximately 1716 BC. In both inscriptions the name of the city is now given as Urbēl.

The Louvre, Paris (AO 2776)

(a) AO 2776   Stele of Šamši-Adad I[34]

A fragmentary stele first shown to Scheil in Mosul and said to come from Sinjar or Mardin. Previously attributed to Dadusha of Eshnunna or to Naram-Sin of Eshnunna, it is now generally accepted that it is to be assigned to Šamši-Adad I.[35] The stele records how in the course of his campaign in the northeast the king attacked and captured Erbil:

> I crossed the river Zab and made a raid on the land of Qabra. I destroyed the harvest of the land and in the month of Magrānu I captured all the fortified cities of the land of Urbel (*ma-a-at ur-bi-e-el*)

33. See Ziegler 2002 2011; Charpin & Ziegler 2003 pp. 92–95.

34. Grayson 1987 (RIMA 1) p. 64 iii'.8; Charpin 2004 pp. 162–165.

35. Previously attributed to Dadusha of Eshnunna by Goetze and to Naram-Sin of Eshnunna by Nagel (for references to the history of attribution see Grayson 1990 p. 562, also Charpin & Ziegler 2003 p. 92).

Chavalas 2006, after Miglus 2003

The Dadusha Stele was damaged during recovery; the line drawing above right interprets the four registers of carved images (Iraq Museum, Baghdad – IM 95200). The iconography of the victorious ruler defeating Būnu-Ištar is similar to that of Šamši-Adad illustrated on the previous page.

(b) IM 95200   **Stele of Dadusha**[36]

Stele found in or near Ešnunna. The text gives the results of the campaign from Dadusha's point of view. In this account of the campaign Dadusha tells how after rampaging through the land of Qabra he came to the city itself, whereupon (viii.10–14):

Corona image of the site of Kurd Qaburstan, a candidate for the site of ancient Qabra. The city walls surrounding the main mound are clearly visible.

> I quickly overpowered their king Būnu-Ištar through the fire of my mighty weapon and immediately sent his head to Eshnunna

The latter part of the stele is most unusual in that it explicitly describes the images carved on it. The section corresponding to Būnu-Ištar (xii.11–12) reads as follows:

> Above the walls of Qabra is Būnu-Ištar king of Urbel (*Ur-bé-él*[ki]) whom I pitilessly caught with my powerful weapon and whom my feet trample.

Middle Assyrian Sources

After the Turukkean rebellion Erbil became independent once more, a status which probably persisted until its absorption in the Mittanni empire. Although nothing is known in detail, the city is likely to have come under Mittanni control no later than the reign of Saustatar and to have been subject to Mittanni approximately 1430–1350 BC. In any case this long history of punctuated autonomy finally comes to an end with the rise of the Middle Assyrian empire in the fourteenth century BC. The Middle Assyrian period (14th-11th centuries BC) was one of the high points in Assyrian history. Under a succession of able kings Assyria expanded to create an empire that stretched to the Euphrates in the west and to the upper Tigris in the north, and also went on to incorporate Babylonia. Unfortunately not a huge amount is known about Erbil (now written Arbail) at this stage. At present we have attestations in two royal inscriptions, a votive inscription and approximately forty-five administrative texts.

36. Grayson 1990 p. 562, Deller 1990, Eidem 1992 p. 16, Ismail & Cavigneaux 2003, Miglus 2003, Charpin 2004 pp. 151–162, Charpin et al. 2004 p. 550f, MacGinnis 2013. The stele is illustrated on the previous page.

Historical sources

Shalmaneser I (1273–1244 BC)[37]

RIMA 1 A.O.77.16 (p.)   Stone slab from Assur

Fragmentary building inscription in which Shalmaneser records "I built the Egašankalamma, the temple of Ištar the Lady of Arbail, my lady, together with its ziggurat"

The ziggurrat of Ur, in its final form dating to the sixth century BC, as restored in the twentieth century. Photo Alison Dingle.

Aššur-rēša-iši (1132–1115 BC)

Chronicle of Aššur-rēša-iši   tablet from Assur[38]

Fragment of an Assyrian chronicle including a note on hostilities between Aššur-rēša-iši and the Babylonian king Ninurta-nadin-šumi. Lines iv.7–20 read:

> That year, Aššur-rēša-iši, king of Assyria, took his soldiers and his chariots and marched on Arbail. Ninurta-nadin-šumi, the king of Karduniaš, heard of the march of Aššur-rēša-iši, king of Assyria. He [recalled?] his troops. The forces and the king of Karduniaš fled [...] with him [...] he sent [...] against [...]

37.   Donbaz & Frame 1983, III.11'.

38.   See Glassner p. 188 No. 14.

Votive inscription

RA 6, 133 (AO 2489)[39]
Bronze statuette found near Lake Urmia.

To Ištar, the great lady who dwells in the Egašankalamma [the temple] of Arbail, [his] mistress, Šamši-bel the scribe of Arbail son of Nergal-nadin-ahi, also scribe, for his life and his wellbeing and the wellbeing of his eldest son has dedicated and presented this statue weighing 1 (+) mina of copper. The name of this statue is Ištar-ana-kaši-uzni ("Ištar, my ear is towards you"). For the life of Aššur-dan king of Assyria, his [king]

date: Aššur-dan I (1178–1133 BC)

The statuette is the only object we have at present which actually came from the Temple of Ištar in Erbil Citadel. It was found near Lake Urmia, where it may have been taken by the Medes as booty following the fall of Nineveh in 612 BC (The Louvre, Paris – AO 2489).

Administrative texts

AfO 10 (1935–6) p.38
No.76 (A 6096b)[40]
limu: Sin-še-ya
date: Aššur-dan I (1178–1133 BC)

1 sheep made (ready) for the palace for the *nu-ga-ti-pi* of Ištar of Arbail

39. M Heuzey Origines Orientales (1891–1915) pl. VIII; Deller Or.Ant. 22 (1983) pp. 17–20); Grayson RIMA 1, pp. 307–8 (A.0.83.2001).

40. Donbaz NTA pl. 18 A. 3187: 6.

AfO 19 pl.7[41]　　　　　　　　　　record of clothing taken to Arbail
VAT 8009

limu's: Ištar-eriš, Aššur-da'issunu, Usat-Marduk
date: late Shalmaneser I (1273–1244 BC)

Al-Rafidan 28, 70　　　　　　　sheep (presumably from Tell Taban) con-
Tab T05A-182　　　　　　　　　sumed in Arbail and Libbu-ali (Assur)

limu: Ištar-[eriš?]
date: Shalmaneser I (1273–1244 BC)

Iraq 30, pl. 60　　　　　　　　　Grain received by PN of Arbail;
TR 3013: 6–7

limu Aššur-zēra-iddina
date: Tukulti-Ninurta I (1243–1207 BC)

JCS 41, 218　　　　　　　　　　12 moulds for glazed bricks given to Šadānu,
A 3310: 9　　　　　　　　　　　the Great Steward (*mašennu rabiu*) […] of
limu: Kidin-Aššur　　　　　　　　Arbail
date: Tiglath-Pileser I (1114–1076 BC)[42]

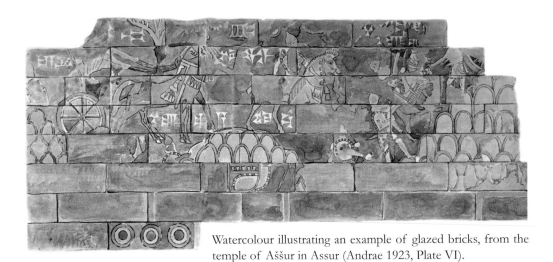

Watercolour illustrating an example of glazed bricks, from the temple of Aššur in Assur (Andrae 1923, Plate VI).

41. See now Faist, AOAT 267, 103.

42. This is the dating of Donbaz and Harrak.

KAJ 178: 16[43] block of copper delivered to Arbail for *ripītu* (meaning uncertain)

limu: Šunu-qardu
date: first decade of Tukulti-Ninurta I (1243–1207 BC)

KAR 152, 36 list of omens, written in the eponymy of Berê, governor of Arbail (*šá-kín* KUR¹ ᵘʳᵘ4-DINGIR)[44]

limu: Berê
date: Aššur-rēša-iši (1132–1115 BC)

MARV 1, 10 document listing issue of arrows "on the day when the king came from Arbail to Libbi-ali (Assur) to perform offerings"

limu: Hiyašāyu
date: first third of the reign of Tiglath-Pileser I (1114–1076 BC)

MARV 1 62 document recording receipt by the temple of Aššur of honey as *ginā'u* contribution of Arbail

limu: Hiyašāyu
date: first third of the reign of Tiglath-Pileser I (1114–1076 BC)

MARV 2, 17 mentions 247 deportees (*nashūte*) from Arbail among
envelope fragment 3 workers in the lower palace of Kar-Tukulti-Ninurta
limu: Abī-ilī, Salmānu-šuma-uṣur
reign: Tukulti-Ninurta I (1243–1207 BC)[45]

MARV 2, 19 document recording receipt of skins of sheep and goats

limu: Usat-Marduk, Enlil-ašared
date: late Shalmaneser I (1273–1244 BC)

---

43. H. Freydank and Cl. Saporetti, *Babu-aha-iddina. Die Texte*. Roma 1989, pp. 40 and 70.

44. For the reading Berê (rather than Barê) see Deller – Postgate, AfO 32, 69b.

45. For the placing of the eponymy of Abī-ilī in year 16 or 17 of Tukulti-Ninurta I see Llop 2010 p. 106.

MARV 2, 21 document recording receipt by the temple of Aššur of *ginā'u* contributions from the provinces, including Arbail

limu: Pauzu
date: Ninurta-apil-ekur (1191–1179 BC)[46]

MARV 3, 8 list of cultic clothing of Ištar of Arbail ordered to be repaired by king Enlil-kudurri-uṣur

limu: Enlil-kudurri-uṣur, *uklu*
date: Enlil-kudurri-uṣur (1196–1192 BC)

MARV 3, 67 bronze axe weighing 1 mina belonging to the palace
(KAJ 298) received by Nanī the palace overseer (*rab ekalli*) of Arbail

limu: -
date: Tiglath-Pileser I (1114–1076 BC)[47]

Bronze axe (British Museum, London – BM 120149).

MARV 5, 1 document recording receipt by the temple of Aššur of *ginā'u* contributions from the provinces, including Arbail

limu: Saggiu (?)
date: Ninurta-apil-Ekurra (1191–1179 BC) (?)

---

46. For the fact that the *limu* Pauzu may date to the reign of Ninurta-apil-ekur see Freydank AfO 33 (2006) p. 218f.
47. Dated by the appearance of Aplīya, *mašennu rabiu* during the reign of Tiglath-Pileser I.

MARV 5, 2 document recording receipt by the temple of Aššur of *ginā'u* contributions from the provinces, including Arbail

limu: Saggiu
date: Ninurta-apil-Ekurra (1191–1179 BC)

MARV 5, 4 document recording receipt by the temple of Aššur of *ginā'u* contributions from the provinces, including Arbail

limu: Aššur-[...]
date: -

MARV 5, 14 document recording receipt by the temple of Aššur of *ginā'u* contributions from the provinces, including Arbail

limu: Aššur-iddin son of Mudammiq-Aššur
date: 12th century BC (pre-Tiglath-Pileser I)

MARV 5, 35 document recording receipt by the temple of Aššur of *ginā'u* contributions from the provinces, including Arbail

limu: Ninurta-apil-ekur, *uklu*
date: Ninurta-apil-ekur (1191–1179 BC)

MARV 5, 58 document recording receipt by the temple of Aššur of *ginā'u* contributions from the provinces; mentions the mayor (*ḫazianu*) of Arbail

limu: -
date: -

MARV 5, 60 Arbail contributes 4 millers out of a total of 47 supplied to the Aššur temple by the provinces (1–4 per province)

limu: -
date: 12th century BC

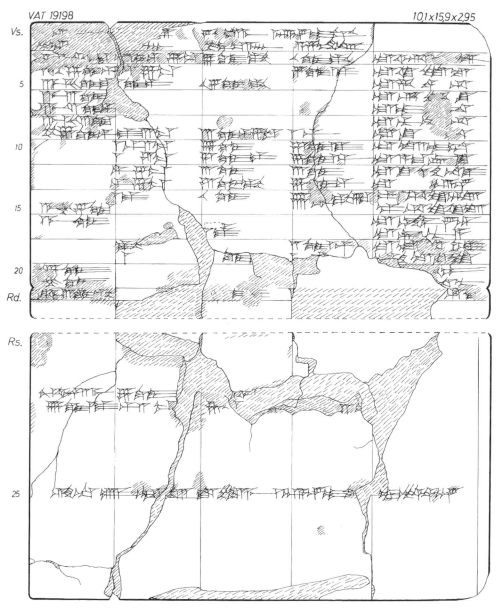

VAT 19198   101x159x295

MARV 5, 14 – tablet from Assur (Vorderasiatisches Museum, Berlin, Germany – VAT 19198).

MARV 5, 67   document recording receipt by the temple of Aššur of *ginā'u* contributions from the provinces, including Arbail

limu: Liptānu
date: Ninurta-apil-ekur (1191–1179 BC)

MARV 6, 2   document recording receipt by the temple of Aššur of *ginā'u* contributions from the provinces, including Arbail

limu's: Pišqiya, Salmānu-zēra-iqiša, Liptānu, Aššur-dān
date: Ninurta-apil-ekur (1191–1179 BC), Aššur-dān (1178–1133 BC)

MARV 6, 5   document recording receipt by the temple of Aššur of *ginā'u* contributions from the provinces, including Arbail

limu: Salmānu-[zēra-iqiša?]
date: [Ninurta-apil-ekur (1191–1179 BC) ?]

MARV 6, 34   document listing consignments of barley from various provinces received by Mār-ṣilliya

limu: -
date: Tiglath-Pileser I[48] (1114–1076 BC)

MARV 6, 42   list of dues of honey, sesame and barley, including those due from the province of Arbail

limu: Erib-Aššur
date: Ninurta-apil-ekur (1191–1179 BC)

MARV 6, 49   document recording receipt by the temple of Aššur of *ginā'u* contributions from the provinces, including Arbail

limu: -
date: 12th century BC

MARV 6, 54   document recording receipt by the temple of Aššur of *ginā'u* contributions from the provinces, including Arbail

limu: Ina-ilīya-allak
date: Tiglath-Pileser I (1114–1076 BC)

---

48.   Llop 2008 p. 183f.

MARV 6, 58	document recording the delivery of sesame from the provinces

limu: -
date: possibly Tiglath-Pileser I (1114–1076 BC)[49]

MARV 6, 78	document recording the delivery of sesame from the provinces

limu: Bel-libūr
date: Tiglath-Pileser I[50] (1114–1076 BC)

MARV 6, 82	document recording receipt by the temple of Aššur of *ginā'u* contributions from the provinces[51]

limu: Pišqīya
date: Ninurta-apil-ekur (1191–1179 BC)

MARV 6, 86	document recording delivery of the barley *ginā'u* contribution of Arbail, together with original envelope

limu: Aššur-šallimšunu, Šamaš-apla-ēreš (tablet)
date: Tiglath-Pileser (1114–1076 BC) (envelope)

MARV 7, 27	list of contributions from the provinces to the temple of Aššur

limu: Adad-rība
date: Enlil-kudurrī-uṣur (1196–1192 BC)

MARV 7, 30	list of contributions from the provinces to the temple of Aššur

limu: -
date: 12th century BC

---

49. Attribution to the time of Tiglath-Pileser I based on the occurrence of the toponym *a-ah* ÍD *hur-ri* (suggestion of Jaume Llop).

50. Llop 2008 p. 183f.

51. Arbail to be restored in l.4.

MARV 7, 55 list of contributions from the provinces to the temple of Aššur

limu: -
date: -

MARV 8, 24 list of contributions from the provinces to the temple of Aššur

limu: Liptānu
date: Ninurta-apil-Ekur (1191–1179 BC)

MARV 8, 40 list of contributions from the provinces to the temple of Aššur

limu: -
date: 12th century BC

MARV 8, 66 list of contributions from the provinces to the temple of Aššur

limu: -
date: 12th century BC

MARV 9, 1 document recording receipt by the temple of Aššur of *ginā'u* contributions from the provinces, including Arbail

limu: Pauzu
date: Possibly Ninurta-apil-ekur (1191–1179 BC)[52]

MARV 9, 2 document recording receipt by the temple of Aššur of *ginā'u* contributions from the provinces, including Arbail

limu: [...]-Aššur (may be the filiation)
date: -

---

52. See MARV 2, No. 21.

MARV 9, 12

document recording receipt by the temple of Aššur of *ginā'u* contributions from the provinces, including Arbail

limu: Salmānu-zēra-iqīša
date: Ninurta-apil-ekur (1191–1179 BC)[53]

MARV 9, 77

administrative text, including information that the Lullu marched in front of the king in (?) Arbail

limu: Tukulti-Ninurta
date: 1243 BC

MARV 9, 80

document recording receipt by the temple of Aššur of *ginā'u* contributions from the provinces, including Arbail

limu: Bēr-naṣir
date: Ninurta-apil-ekur (1191–1179 BC)

MDOG 134, 74
(Ass. 2001.D-2034: 2)
limu: Aššur-šumu-lēšir
date: Shalmaneser I (1273–1244 BC)

Delivery of *simdu* flour from Arbail as the *iškāru* of a certain Šamaš-[...] the *alaḫḫinu ša karkadinnē*

Weidner 1959 pl. XI
VAT 16451 (p. 45, 39E)
limu: -
date: Tukulti-Ninurta I (1243–1207 BC)

Fragmentary text possibly concerning overland trade conducted by the palace;[54] [Ar]-ba-il is mentioned in l.4'.

---

53. Llop ZA 98, p. 24.

54. See Freydank Bi.Or. 35 p. 227 and MARV 3 p. 136 (ad No. 78).

Neo-Assyrian Sources

Following the contraction of the Middle Assyrian state and a period of reduced circumstances, in the late tenth century the kings of Assyria embarked upon a resurgence which was to take Assyria to its maximum dimensions. The end was also rapid. Following the death of Ashurbanipal the empire began to quickly unravel. In 612 BC Nineveh fell to a coalition of the Medes and Babylonians. For a few years a reduced state staggered on centered around a capital at Harran, but by 605 BC at the latest the Assyria had finally come to an end. In both number and variety the Neo-Assyrian period gives us by far the richest data on the history of Erbil.

Historical Texts

Chronicles

On four occasions the Eponym Chronicle lists governors of Arbail as the year's eponym.[55]

entry for 787 BC: Şil-Ištar, of Arbail, to Media; Nabû entered the new temple

entry for 784 BC: Marduk-šarru-uşur, of Arbail, to Hubuškia

entry for 759 BC: Pān-Aššur-lāmur, of Arbail, revolt in Guzana; plague

entry for 702 BC: Nabû-le'i, governor of Arbail

Note also that the scribe of one of the manuscripts of the Assyrian Royal Chronicle was a scribe of the temple of Ištar (although it was actually written in Assur).[56]

King Lists

JNES 13 p.229 iv.35   Khorsabad King List   Tiglath-Pileser III
Colophon stating that the tablet is a copy from Aššur by the hand of Kandalānu, a scribe of the temple of Arbail; dated to the second eponymy of Adad-bel-ukin governor of Aššur.

---

55. Millard 1994 p. 58; Glassner 2005 p. 168 1.32'.35', p. 170 1.60', p. 174 1.17.

56. Glassner 2005 p. 144 (No. 5).

Aššur-dan II (934–912 BC)

RIMA II Aššur-dan II A.O.98.1 l.40 (p. 134)

At the end of his campaign against Katmuhu Aššur-dan recounts "Kundibhalle king of the land of Katmuhu, I brought to Assyria (and) in the city of Arbail I flayed (him and) draped his skin over the wall [.....]".

Ashurnasirpal II (883–859 BC)

RIMA II Ashurnasirpal II A.O.101.1 l.67–68 (p. 198)
RIMA II Ashurnasirpal II A.O.101.17 l.88–89 (p. 242)

In the course of the campaigning undertaken at the beginning of his reign, Ashurnasirpal recounts: "Bubu son of Babua, the ruler of the city ofNištun, I flayed in Arbail and draped his skin over the wall".

Inscribed stele of Ashurnasirpal II (British Museum, London – BM 118805)

Shalmaneser III (858–824 BC)

RIMA III Shalmaneser III A.O.102.6 ii.2 (p. 36)
RIMA III Shalmaneser III A.O.102.8 l.5' (p. 45)

After his campaign against Aramu of Urartu in the third year of his reign, for his return Shalmaneser states "From the pass of Mount Kirruru I emerged before the city of Arbail".

RIMA III Shalmaneser III A.O.102.17.59–60 (p. 87)[57]

This campaign is unusual in that it is also recorded in a verse composition which first of all mentions the deeds of Ashurnasirpal before narrating Shalmaneser's campaign against Urartu; from the reference to the field marshal Aššur-bēl-kala this has been identified as the campaign of the third year. After returning from Urartu Shalmaneser records how "With steadfast heart I entered the Egašankalamma and [celebrated] the festival of the Lady of Arbail in Milkia".

RIMA III Shalmaneser III A.O.102.28 l.42 (p. 104)

In his thirteenth year the king again campaigned against Aramu of Urartu:
"I entered the pass of the land of Enzi and came out before Arbail".

RIMA III Shalmaneser III A.O.102.6 iii.58 (p. 40)

And then three years later:
"In my sixteenth year I set out from Arbail, crossed mount Kullar and established a fortress in the interior of the land of Zamua".

Šamši-Adad V (823–811 BC)

RIMA III Šamši-Adad V A.O.103.1.i.49 (p. 183)

Arbail listed among the 27 cities which joined the rebellion of Aššur-danin-apli against Shalmaneser III and which were brought under submission by Šamši-Adad V.

---

57. Lambert 1961 (STT 43) = SAA 3 17.

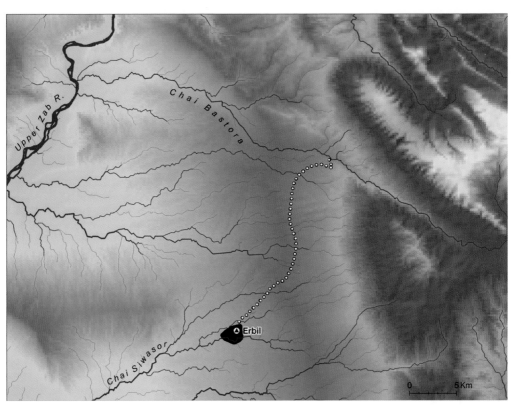

Course of Sennacherib's underground canal from the Bastora valley to the centre of Erbil (Courtesy Jason Ur).

Sennacherib (704–681 BC)

Inscription of Sennacherib on the Bastura river
Sumer 2 (1946), 50–52
Sumer 3 (1947), 23–25[58]

I Sennacherib, king of the world, king of Assyria, dug three rivers from the Hani mountains, the mountains which are above the city of Erbil and added to them the waters of the springs which are on the right and left sides of the rivers. Then I dug a canal into the middle of the city of Erbil, the abode of the goddess Ištar, the exalted lady, and I caused their courses to be straight.

The silted up entrance to the channel in the Bastora Valley; unfortunately the inscription was stolen in the early 1990s.

There is a revetment of massive coursed stonework on either side of the entrance, which is angled to receive the water from the river.

Areas of massive stone cobbles probably represent the paving of the canalisation of the three rivers which Sennacherib refers to in his inscription (photos – Stafford Clarry.)

58.   Cf. Frahm 1997 p. 159.

Esarhaddon (680–669 BC)

Esarhaddon carried out a major refurbishment of the temple of Ištar, recorded in his cylinder inscriptions and in the "Letter to God".

Esarhaddon cylinder Kalah A

In the cylinder composed to record the building of the southwest palace in Nimrud Esarhaddon also records, amongst his other deeds:[59]

> He clothed Egašankalamma, the temple of Ištar of Arbail, his lady, with electrum alloy (*zahalû*) and made it shine like the day. He had fashioned lions, lion headed *anzû*-birds, bulls and naked heroes (*lahmu*) and griffins (*kurību*) of silver and gold and set them up in the entrance of its gates.

British Museum, London
(BM 131129)

Massive alabaster relief from Khorsabad
depicting a hero subduing a lion
(The Louvre, Paris – AO 19862)

59. Borger 1956 p. 33, Leichty 2011 p. 117; cf. Wiseman Iraq 14 (1952) p. 54 BM 131129 ND 1126 line 8; note that Wiseman translates *na-'-i-ri* as "dolphins". For the translations of *lahmu* and *kurību* see Wiggerman 1992 pp. 164–166 and p. 181 (quoting Reade BaM 10 41: unwinged lion centaur) respectively.

Sammeltext

In this redaction of his achievements Esarhaddon gives a detailed description of his rebuilding of the Egašankalamma:[60]

> I covered [Egašankalamma the temple of Ištar] which is in Erbil with silver and gold so that it shone like the day. I fashioned [...] of bronze and attached them to the bolts of its gates. I built [...]-*māte* inside it and surrounded [...]. Since Ištar my Lady had made my kingdom bigger than that of the kings my forefathers I (in turn) expanded its dimensions. [I *renovated*] the *akītu* house in the open countryside, the house of merry making, and restored its rites. [I *finished*] that [temple] with baked bricks, haematite and lapis lazuli and built it with lofty cedar beams and [...] its [...]. On the seventeenth day of Ululu I [...] hastened to bring their offerings before them. With deep insight and profound wisdom I settled them in the *akītu* house. [....], 10 sheep, 10 birds, 7 homers of wine, 4 homers of [...], groats beer (*hašlatu*), [all] this I established before them for the table of their divinities in the *akītu* house in the open countryside.

Letter to God

In the "Letter to God" Esarhaddon also describes how after the conquest of Shubria he distributed Shubrian captives among the temples of Assyria, including the temple of Ištar of Arbail along with the temples of Aššur, Ninlil, Šerua, [...], Ištar of Nineveh and Nusku[61] and that he gave prisoners from Shubria to the citizens of Nineveh, Calah, Kilizu and Arbail: "I filled the whole of the land of Assyria like a quiver. The remainder I divided up like sheep among my palaces, my magnates, the entourage of my palaces and the citizens of Nineveh, Kalhu, Kilizi and Arbail".[62]

---

60. Borger 1956 p. 95, Leichty 2011 p. 84.

61. Letter to God II.iii.8f (Borger 1956 p. 95).

62. Borger 1995 p. 106, Leichty 2011 p. 84.

Prism A   (redaction of 643 BC)

This edition of the annals of Ashurbanipal contains the following entry from the course of the king's fourth campaign against the Mannean king Ahšeri:[63]

> Ahšeri who did not fear my lordship, Aššur and Ištar handed him over to the hands of his servants, who rebelled against him and threw his corpse into the street of his city, in accordance with the word of Ištar who dwells in Arbail, which she had spoken at the outset: "I will bring about the death of Ahšeri, the king of the land of the Manneans, as I said" – (Ištar) handed him over to the hands of his servants.

In the course of his eighth campaign against Elam Ashurbanipal recounts:[64]

> My troops saw the Idide, a wild river and were afraid to cross it. In the night Ištar who dwells in Arbail sent a vision to my troops. She spoke to them thus: "I will go before Ashurbanipal the king whom I created with my own hands". My troops rejoiced at this dream and crossed the river Idide safely.

And the following entry from the king's ninth campaign against Uaite' the king of the Arabs:[65]

> Ištar of Arbail who is clothed in fire and bears an aegis (*melammu*) rained down fire over the land of the Arabs

Prism B   (redaction of 649 BC)

This edition of the annals of Ashurbanipal contains a detailed account of the king's seventh campaign against Teuman king of Elam:[66]

> In the month of Ab, at the appearance of the Bow star, (during) the festival of the great queen, the daughter of Enlil, I was present to worship her great divinity in Arbail the city beloved of her heart. Here I was brought the news of the attack of the Elamite who had risen up against me in contravention of the will of the gods, as follows: "Teu-

---

63.   Borger 1996 p. 35 Prisma A iii 4–9.

64.   Borger 1996 pp. 50–51 Prisma A v 95–103.

65.   Borger 1996 p. 68 Prisma A ix 79–81.

66.   Borger 1996 pp. 99–100 Prisma B v 15–76.

man, whom Ištar deprived of his reason, has said: 'I will not give up until I come and fight a battle with him' ". It was on account of this insolence which Teuman, king of Elam, addressed to me, that I approached the exalted warrior Ištar, took my stand in her presence, bowed down and with my tears flowing implored her divinity: "O Lady of Arbail, I am Ashurbanipal, king of Assyria, the creation of your hands, whom Aššur king of the gods thy father desired and whose name he called to restore the sanctuaries of Assyria and renew their rites, to guard their secrets and to make their hearts glad. I have sought out your sanctuary and come to worship your divinity. Now this Teuman king of Elam who does not value the gods is setting in motion his whole military establishment in order to make war on my forces. O thou Lady of Ladies, goddess of war, lady of battle, who gives counsel to the great gods her fathers, who spoke favourably before Aššur, the father who begot you, (so that) by the lifting of his pure eyes he chose me to be king: because Teuman king of Elam who has rebelled against Aššur king of the gods, thy father, has <withheld his> tribute, mustered his troops, prepared himself for battle and sharpened his weapons in order to march on Assyria: may you, heroic one among the gods, in the midst of battle drive him away like a pack animal! Call up against

Prism F (the redaction of 646 BC) includes another version of the text describing Ashurbanipal's campaign against Elam in 657 BC (The Louvre, Paris – AO 19939).

him a tempest and an evil wind!" Ištar heard my anxious sighs and said to me "Do not Fear!" and made me confident. "Because of your supplication and your eyes filled with tears I have had mercy!" In the course of that same night when I had turned to her, a seer had a vision in his sleep. When he woke he reported to me this nocturnal vision which Ištar has sent him: "Ištar who dwells in Arbail came in. She had quivers hanging left and right[67] and held a bow in her arm and a sharp sword drawn for doing battle. You stood in front (of her) and she talked with you like the mother who bore (you). Ištar, exalted among the gods, addressed you and gave you the following message: 'You saw a vision of war. Wherever my face is turned I will go forth'. You said to her 'Where you go, I will go with you, O lady of ladies'. She repeated to you (these instructions): 'You should remain here in your place. Eat food, drink beer, provide music, honour my divinity until I go and carry out this work and cause you to attain your heart's desire. Your face shall not grow pale, your feet shall not grow weary, your strength shall not fail

---

67. The quivers hanging either side of Ištar are also mentioned in a fragmentary section of the Nergal-Laṣ inscription (K 2631+): Borger 1996 p. 84 l.50.

in the midst of battle' In her kindly embrace she clasped you and protected your whole body. A flame burst forth before her. Furiously she set out. Against Teuman king of Elam, against whom she was enraged, she turned her face."

In the course of his eighth campaign Ashurbanipal recounts the following:[68]

Dunanu and Samgunu, the sons of Bel-iqīša of the Gambulu (tribe), whose forefathers had disturbed the kings my forefathers and now himself was causing disturbances during my reign, I brought to Arbail to sing my praise forever. In Arbail I ripped out the tongues and flayed the skin of Mannu-ki-ahhē the deputy of Dunanu and Nabû-uṣalli, the prefect of the city of Gambulu, who had spoken a great slander against my gods.

Prism T   (redaction of 645 BC)

This edition contains this summary statement:[69]

"I adorned the Egašankalamma in silver and gold and filled (it) with splendour."

IIIR 16 No. 4

Another version of the Teuman sequence appears in the Ištar Temple Inscription from Nineveh:[70]

[......] Ištar the exalted lady who dwells in Arbail [......] who subdues [......] Ashurbanipal, for whom the going out [......] she gave a righteous sceptre, who makes wide [......] called by Dilbat, daughter of Enlil, lady of [......] whom Ištar, daughter of Sin [......] for the subjugation of (his) enemies [......] in the month of Abu, the month of the appearance of the Bow star, (at) the feast [of the honoured queen] I, Ashurbanipal king of Assyria raised my clean hands [to her exalted divinity]. It was on account of this insolence which Teuman, king of Elam, addressed to me, that I approached the exalted Ištar, took my stand in her presence, bowed down and implored her divinity: "O Lady of Arbail, I am Ashurbanipal, king of Assyria, the creation of your hands, whom Aššur king of the gods your father commanded to restore the sanctuaries of Assyria and complete the rebuilding of the cities of Akkad. I have sought out your sanctuary and come to worship your divinity. Now this Teuman king of Elam who does not esteem the gods is setting in motion his whole military establishment in order to make war on me.

68. Borger 1996 p. 107 Prisma B vi 77–87.
69. Borger 1996 p. 140 & 206 (T II 7–8).
70. Borger 1996 p. 101f.

K 8016[71]

The events surrounding the campaign against Teuman are also narrated in a literary tablet composed for Ashurbanipal. After hearing Teuman's insolent message Ashurbanipal states:[72]

I opened my hands (in supplication) to [Ištar, the Lady of Arbail], saying "I am Ashurbanipal whom [your] own father [Aššur] engendered. I have [come] to worship you. Why is Teuman falling upon me?

After the completion of the campaign the text goes on to say:[73]

[They brought Teuman and] his family in [neckstocks before] Mulissu and the Lady of [Arbail] and put him to the sword.

K 891

Inscription on a clay tablet from Erbil which opens with a summary of Ashurbanipal's work in Arbail:[74]

Arbail the residence of Ištar, the house of festivals [......] the wall of which had not been built since time immemorial and [its outer wall] had not been completed: I built its wall and completed its outer wall [and filled it] with splendour. With gold (and) copper I made the temple of Ištar, my Lady, shine like the day [......]. I adorned and set up the standards at the gate of the temple of Ištar. I renewed the delapidated Milkia, the countryside palace residence of Ištar. I constructed its *akītu* house. I completely rebuilt the city. I commenced with lamentation and weeping that the enemy had destroyed it and in jubilation I rebuilt it.

The remaining part of the tablet deals with Ashurbanipal's erection of new standards in the temple of Nergal in Tarbiṣu, his appointment of two of his brothers to priesthoods, his establishing of offerings to his predecessors and a lamentation of his woes.

---

71. Bauer Ashurbanipal pl. 45, SAA 3 31.

72. SAA 3 31, 14–17.

73. SAA 3 31, rev. 8–9.

74. Streck *Assurbanipal* pl. XLVf 248ff; according to the original publication in IR pl. 8 No. 2 the tablet is from Erbil; this statement might however only be made on the content of the text.

Erbil in the Cuneiform Sources

Three alabaster panels from the South West Palace, Room XXXIII, in Nineveh, although damaged, vividly portray Ashurbanipal's victory celebrations in Erbil in 657 BC. Ranks of soldiers stand in front of and behind the king, who can be seen in his chariot in the right-hand panel. The left-hand panel depicts what may be Mannu-ki-ahhē, the deputy of Dunanu, and Nabû-uṣalli, the prefect of the city of Gambulu, having their tongues ripped out; the scene immediately above certainly shows them being flayed alive. Immediately to the right soldiers proffer severed heads to Ashurbanipal. Two noble ambassadors from Urartu, distinguished by caps with tassels, witness the scene (British Museum, London – BM 124802, a,b,c).

The contemporary relief of Erbil, originally from Nineveh, shows the double walls of the lower city, and above that the walls of the Citadel and its arched gate, outside of which there is a pillar-shaped incense burner with a crennelated top. Rising above the Citadel walls is the Temple of Ištar and flanking the gate are two tall standards, which Ashurbanipal states that he renewed. Showing just above the Citadel walls, on the right-hand side of the gate, a ceremony is in progress outside the gate of the Temple of Ištar, although the scene is damaged and difficult to discern. Above the Citadel gate a figure, presumably Ashurbanipal himself, is pourinig a libation over a severed human head, presumably that of Teuman king of Elam, which has been placed in front of an offering table, the turned legs of which can be clearly seen (discussed in Albenda 1980). This ceremony can be compared to the libation ceremoney depicted on p. 87. The cuneiform inscription ^{uru}4-DINGIR – inscribed on the wall of the Citadel - identifies the city depicted as Erbil (The Louvre, Paris – AO 19914).

Ištar Temple Inscription (Nineveh)

This is Ashurbanipal's inscription for the temple of Ištar in Nineveh, known from multiple copies. It summarises much of the king's work including the following with respect to Arbail:[75]

> I rebuilt the Egašankalamma [the temple of Ištar of Arbail] and clothed its walls in gold.

Epigraphs prepared for reliefs

(1) I Ashurbanipal, king of Assyria, made sumptuous offerings in Milkia and celebrated the festival of Šatru. At that time Dunanu was bound hand and foot in iron chains and brought to me.[76]

(2) I Ashurbanipal, king of Assyria, after I had made offerings to Šatru and carried out the festival of the *akītu* house and grasped the reins of Ištar, I made a triumphal entry into Arbail accompanied by Dunanu, Samgunu and Aplāya and the severed head of Teuman king of Elam, whom Ištar had given into my hands.[77]

(3) With the decapitated head of Teuman king of Elam I took the road to Arbail rejoicing.[78]

(4) I am Ashurbanipal, king of the universe, king of Assyria, who with the help of Aššur and Ištar, my lords, have conquered my enemies and achieved all the desires of my heart: Rusa king of Urartu heard of the might of Aššur my lord and the fear of my majesty overwhelmed him. He sent his nobles to greet me in Arbail. I presented to them Nabû-damiq (and) Umbara, the nobles of Elam, with the tablets bearing (their) insolent messages.[79]

(5) I had Dunanu, Samgunu and Aplāya chained to a bear in the western and eastern gates for the population to marvel at.[80]

75. Line 42: Borger 1996 p. 291.

76. Borger 1996 p. 302 line 20; Russel 1999 p. 162.

77. Borger 1996 p. 305, line 34 III 47; Russel 1999 p.162.

78. Borger 1996 p. 307 B 3–4 = E rev.7–8; Russell 1999 p. 162; "Ištar of Arba[il]" is also mentioned in a fragmentary context in Borger 1996 p. 304 B rev.2. Drawings of the reliefs with the procession to Arbail (BM 2007,6024.575 and 2007,6024.576) are illustrated in Russell 1999, pp. 183–4.

79. Borger 1996 p. 307 E (I R No. 8 No. 1, III R 37 1–37), Russel 1999 p. 163.

80. Borger 1996 p. 303, Russel 1999 p. 163; as suggested by Reade 1979 p. 99, this is more likely to be Arbail than Nineveh.

Grants/edicts

SAA 12 89   (Bauer Asb. pl. 50)[81]   Esarhaddon/Ashurbanipal

A fragment of a royal votive gift to Ištar of Arbail dating to the reign of either Esarhaddon or Ashurbanipal including the establishment (inter alia) of 2 litres of wine
per day and 10 sheep per month in the Egašankalamma. The introduction, which is
broken, mentions Raṣappa, Bit-Zamani and Uppumu and the implication may be that
these (and other) provinces were responsible for the delivery of these offerings; bakers, brewers, cooks and gardener(s) are also mentioned. All this is in addition to the
confirmation of the decrees of grants of earlier kings.

> [......] Raṣappa, Bit Zamani [......] ...... the province of Uppumu [......] gardeners, bak-
> ers, cooks, brewers [......] I [gave] to Ištar who dwells in Arbail, my Lady [......] these
> sheep which I gave as a gift [......] 2 litres of wine per day and 10 sheep per month
> [......] I established forever [before her] in the Egašankalamma [for the preservation
> of my life], the length of my days, the endurance of my reign, the overthrow of my
> enemies. I increased and confirmed [the decrees of the king]s my forefathers. May
> your heart be glad, may your spirit [shine ......] choice beer. May you continually bless
> my reign [......]. May you decree [as my fate] the attaining of (my) heart's desires! [......]
> intercede for me [with ...... Accept] the *bursaggu* offerings which I have brought before
> [you .....] fires [.....] I dedicated [.....]

SAA 12 50   (ADD 742)   Ashurbanipal (?)

Land grant including a number of farms with their personnel in the district (*halzu*) of
Arbail; a house and a half vegetable plot opposite the Nineveh Gate in Arbail; and
a field and two vineyards in the centre of town in the best part of Arbail (*ina* SAG
^{uru}4-*il*).

SAA 12 69   (NARGD 42)   Adad-Nerari III
Edict concerning temple expenditures, mentions the prefect (*šakin māti*) of Arbail
(rev.17).

SAA 12 71–72   (NARGD 46–47)   Adad-Nerari III
Edict concerning offerings of the temple of Aššur: details sheep, wine, oil, flour,
honey, pomegranates and apples, apparently from the areas of Burali and Arbail.

---

81. Borger 1956 p. 97, 119 (Sm 1730).

SAA 12 87[82] (KAV 39) Sennacherib

List of 41 people from Arbail dedicated by Sennacherib to the god Zababa to be tillers (*qātinūte*) following an oracular enquiry to Šamaš and Adad.

SAA 12 93 (ADD 641) Ashurbanipal

Dedication by a eunuch's shield bearer of his son to Ninurta of Calah; the curse formulae included the entry "May Ištar who resides in Arbail clothe him in leprosy".

SAA 12 97 (ND 6207, NARGD 37) no date preserved

Dedication of people to Nabû; the curse formulae included the entry "May Ištar who resides in Arbail fill him with leprosy and cut off his entrance to temple and palace".

Votive Inscription

Til Barsip Stele

Inscription on a stele depicting Ištar standing on a lion:[83]

> To Ištar who lives in Arbail, his mistress, Aššur-dūr-pānīya, governor of Kar-Shalmaneser, has dedicated (this stele) for his life

The stele, dedicated by a provincial governor, represents the cult statue of Ishtar in the Egašankalamma in Erbil Citadel and illustrates the widespread popularity of her cult (The Louvre, Paris – AO 11503).

82. Cf. Frahm 1997 p. 241.

83. AO 11503, Radner 2006.

Administrative texts

AfO Beiheft 6 p. 62   TH 112   625 BC
Loan of silver, capital of Ištar of Arbail, belonging to Adad-milki-ilā'ī.

AfO Beiheft 6 p. 63   TH 113   not dated
Loan of silver, capital of Ištar of Arbail, belonging to Adad-milki-ilā'ī.

As14967   Deller 1984 p. 228–22   no information available
Letter recording the verdict of a case heard in Arbail in which 2 minas of silver were awarded in a dispute concerning some textiles (*na-ẓa-ad-sa-te*) and a yoke of oxen.

As09644o   (Assur)   Post 648 BC
Loan of silver of Ištar of [Arbail] (*limmu* Bel-ah-uṣur).

As14325ab   (Assur)   date broken
Loan of silver of Ištar of Arbail (*limmu* Nabû-[......]).

As15452a*   (Assur)   Post 648 BC
Loan of silver of Ištar of Arbail (*limmu* Zababa-eriba).

CTN II 17   ND 496   783 BC
Land sale in which the penalty clauses include dedicating 7 male hierodules (ˡᵘSUHUR. LÁ.MEŠ) and 7 female hierodules (ˢSUHUR.LÁ.MEŠ) to Ištar of Arbail.

CTN II 91   ND 262   797 BC
Legal document ratifying the clearing of a debt, witnesses include a weaver from Arbail.

CTN III 86.19   ND 10005   Tiglath-Pileser III/Sargon
List of officials serving provincial cities, including a certain Bel-emuranni serving the cities of Isana, Šahupa and Arbail.

CTN III 87   ND 10009   8th or 7th century BC

Large tablet of *ilkakāte* payments which the deputy steward of (or for) Arbail delivered to the palace. The payments include grapes, juniper and other aromatics, *titipu*-fruit, copper, leeks, pomegranates, grain, cakes and pistachios; paid by the brewer of the campaign, the *karkadinnu* official in charge of leather bags, the officials in charge of salted meats, the official in charge of *akūsu*-soups/sauces, the official in charge of *billu* (beer), the official in charge of aromatic plants, the mace bearer for ambassadors, officials of the queen and other officials whose titles are missing or damaged.

CTN III 93.11   ND 10011   Sargon (?)

Text recoding the issue or allocation of large amounts of copper, either to various shrines in different cities or to various shrines in Kalhu from different cities. 72 talents 2 minas are associated with Arbail.

CTN III 97.3   ND 10014   Sargon (?)

List of chariots including 5 with (?) copper in the *kalzu* district of Arbail.

CTN III 102.iii.21.26   ND 10019   711 BC

List of horses for the army including an entry of 26 from the section commanders (*rab kiṣri*) of Arbail and 4 from a certain Kakku-ereš of Arbail, to be repaid.

CTN III 108.ii.24   ND 9910+   710–708 BC

List of horses for the army including a section listing the contributions of 7 individuals of (the contingent of) Arbail.

CTN V p. 107   ND 2402   Sargon

Letter to the king from Šulmu-Bel reporting that the chiefs of the fortresses of the land of the Urartians, whom the governor of Calah brought, are in Arbail.

CTN V p. 224   ND 2616   Tiglath-Pileser III/Sargon

Letter concerning people who have no food, mentioning the governor of Arbail.

DM 9/41/97 Diyarbakir 8th/7th century BC[84]
Loan of silver, first fruits of Ištar of Arbail (*limmu* Nabû-šar-uṣur).

Faist StAT 3 105 As14067c 634 BC
Sale of a slave belonging to Assur and Ištar of Arbail.

Faist StAT 3 109 As14724b 655 BC
Loan of half a mina of silver of Ištar of Arbail.

Iraq 15 p. 143 ND 3440 652 BC
Loan of silver according to the standard of Arbail.

Iraq 15 p. 152 ND 3455 no date
Tablet listing amounts of silver and adding at the end 1 "Aramean duck" (KUR.
GI.MUŠEN *ar-ra-mi-i*) from Arbail.

Iraq 16 p. 38 ND 2308 no date
Redemption of a woman given as a pledge; Ištar of Arbail mentioned in curse formulae.

Iraq 16 p. 45 ND 2336 658 BC
Loan of silver, first fruits of Ištar of Arbail, belonging to Izbu.

Iraq 23 p. 31 ND 2465 no date
Arbail listed along with other towns and villages making payments of grain to the *rab
danibati* (chief victualler).

Iraq 23 p. 34 ND 2491 no date
Fragmentary list of equids.

Iraq 23 p. 36 ND 2499 no date
Fragmentary list of equids, chariots, shields and bows.

84. There are three eponyms called Nabû-šar-uṣur: one for 786 BC, one for 682 BC and one post-
canonical: see Millard 1994 p. 107.

Iraq 23 p. 40   ND 2640   no date
Administrative document detailing commodities and livestock from various cities and mentioning cattle, sheep and cloth from the palace belonging to Arbail (under the jurisdiction of) the governor (*bēl pīhāti*) of Arbail.

Iraq 23 p. 41   ND 2650   no date
Administrative document listing amounts of silver for the manufacture of tableware, including 10 ⅓ minas of silver from Arbail.

Iraq 23 p. 44   ND 2694   no date
Administrative document detailing amounts of an unspecified metal, including an allocation for the *bīt akīti* of Arbail.

Iraq 23 p. 46   ND 2728   no date
Fragment of a land census including 7 villages in the district (*qannu*) of Arbail.

Iraq 23 p. 53   ND 2789   no date
Directions for the setting up of offerings tables with cups and with offerings of bread, honey, oil and meat for the ceremony of the changing of the divine clothes at Milkia.

Alabaster relief from Nineveh depicting Ashurbanipal pouring a libation over slain lions in front of an offering table (British Museum, London – BM 124886). This scene can be compared to the less well preserved depiction of a libation ceremony outside the gate of the Temple of Ištar (p. 80). In that scene the king is also carrying a bow and is pouring a libation in front of an offering table and has fan-bearers behind him. In this scene he is faced by two musicians playing horizontal forearm harps, but in the Erbil scene two figures directly face him across the offering table.

Iraq 23 p. 54   ND 2791   no date

List of payments of grain including 70 homers from Arbail.

Iraq 23 p. 55f   ND 2803   no date

Large tablet listing the allocations of grain for personnel: obv.ii.21' lists 8 homers of the governor (*bēl pıhāti*) of Kilizi, of Arbail; and Arbail is also mentioned in the fragmentary entry rev.ii.8.

Iraq 25 p. 89   BT 101   710 BC

Loan of half a mina of silver from a merchant of Ištar of Arbail.

Iraq 25 p. 93   BT 113   697 BC.

Loan of copper, capital of Ištar of Arbail, belonging to Šumma-ilu.

Iraq 25 p. 95   BT 117   686 BC.

Undertaking to supply grain for the *lahmu* of the *qarītu* of Arbail.

Iraq 25 p. 96   BT 120   early 7th century BC

Loan of silver, capital of Ištar of Arbail, belonging to Šumma-ilu.

Iraq 25 p. 98   BT 128   682 BC

Loan of silver, capital of Ištar of Arbail.

JSS 28 p. 155   MAH 16602   no date

Loan of silver, first fruits of Ištar of Arbail, belonging to Nanuni.

MAss 112   (Assur)   seventh century BC[85]

Loan of silver of Ištar of Arbail (*limmu* Kanūnāya).

O 3708   Ma'allanate   644 BC

Document recording the verdict on a case about a dispute concerning a field; the penalty clauses include the stipulation that any future violator will have to give a *kezru* (oblate) to Ištar of Arbail (*limmu* Nabû-šar-uṣur *rab ša rēši*).

O 3712   Ma'allanate   697 BC

Sale of a field adjoining the dais of Ištar of Arbail (*limmu* Nabû-dūr- uṣur).

RA 24 p. 116 No. 4. rev.7   (Nineveh)   617 BC

Barley loan, silver equivalent calculated as "silver of Arbail".

Rafidain 17   p. 255 No. 23   IM 119287   after 648 BC

Loan of 4½ minas of silver, first fruits of Ištar of Arbail, belonging to Aššur-mudammiq. The eponym is the post-canonical Upaqu-ana-Arbail.

SAA 1 39.10   (ABL 1177)   reign of Sargon

Letter in which the author asks permission to petition the king to go to Arbail.

SAA 1 146.6   (ABL 136)   reign of Sargon

Letter from Šamaš-upahhir concerning work in Milkia.[86]

SAA 1 147.4   (ABL 526)   reign of Sargon

Letter from city rulers concerning work in Milkia.

---

85. There are three eponyms called Kanūnāya: one for 671 BC, one for 666 BC and one post-canonical: see Millard 1994 pp. 97–98.

86. Milkia is also mentioned in SAA 1 125.4.

SAA 1 135.7   (ABL 179)   reign of Sargon

Letter in which the author Amar-ili reports to the king that he and the governor of Arbail inspected a writing board and divided up the inheritance of a certain Mardû evenly among his sons.

Alabaster relief from Nineveh depicting two military scribes taking notes after a victory. One is using a writing board; the other (a eunuch) is writing on a scroll, probably in Aramaic (British Museum, London – BM 124955)

SAA 1 149.7   (CT 53 108)   reign of Sargon

Letter in which the author Aššur-šarru-ibni reports that the governor of Arbail has 120 men who did not go on campaign and complains that he will not give them to him.

SAA 1 155.10   (ABL 218)   reign of Sargon

Letter concerning Philistine troops in Arbail.

SAA 1 160.rev.13   (ABL 843)   reign of Sargon

Statement by Tariba-Issar that he will collect grain in Adian and Arbail if ordered and recording grain delivered to the governor of Arbail.

SAA 1, 170.4.rev.6   (CT 53 333)   reign of Sargon

Letter concerning deliveries of barley including a consignment from the governor of Arbail.

SAA 5 136 (ABL 891) reign of Sargon

Arbail listed as the terminal point on the itinerary of tribute being sent to Assyria by Urzanâ of Muṣaṣir.[87]

SAA 5 149.15 (ABL 1273) reign of Sargon

Letter reporting that the deputy of the palace herald has been oppressing the land of Hargu and has taken receipt in Arbail of an extortionate amount of silver from their ruler.

SAA 5 151.6 (CT 53 637) reign of Sargon

Letter to the king mentionimg Arbail and a palace.

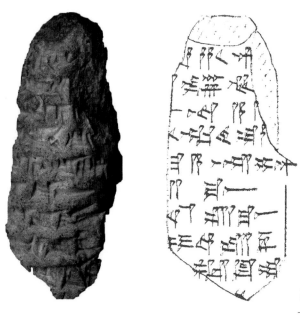

British Museum, London
– K 15291

SAA 5 152.e.27 (ABL 784) reign of Sargon

Letter in which the author Aššur-alik-pani commits to bring his infantry, cavalry and chariotry to meet the king in Arbail.

87.   Following the restoration proposed by Lanfranchi 1995 pp. 130–131.

SAA 6 3.13 (ADD 492) Tiglath-Pileser III/Sargon
Slave sale: the punishment for any future litigator is to pay 5 minas of silver and 1 mina of gold to Ištar of Arbail.

SAA 6 7.e.17 (ADD 180) Tiglath-Pileser III/Sargon
Slave sale: the punishment for any future litigator is to pay 10 minas of silver and 1 mina of gold to Ištar of Arbail and to return the money tenfold to its owners.

SAA 6 34.rev.2 (ADD 234) 709 BC
Slave sale: the punishment for any future litigator is to pay [x] minas of silver and 1 mina of gold to Ištar of Arbail and to return the money tenfold to its owners.

SAA 6 157.2 (ADD 43) 687 BC
Loan of 31 minas of copper belonging to Ištar of Arbail.

SAA 6 159.4 (ADD 353) 687 BC
Sale of a vacant lot behind the city of Arbail.

SAA 6 176.8 (ADD 376) reign of Sennacherib
Land sale: the punishment for any future litigator is to pay 1 mina of silver and 2 minas of gold to Ištar of Arbail and to return the money tenfold to its owners.

SAA 6 184.2 (ADD 108) reign of Sennacherib
Loan of 1 talent and 3 minas of copper, first fruits of Ištar of Arbail, belonging to Sin-[remanni] at the disposal of Gab-[...].

SAA 6 209.rev.8 (ADD 617) reign of Esarhaddon
Sale of a house, field and threshing floor in which the mayor (*ḫazānu*) of Arbail appears as a witness.

SAA 6 210.rev.1   (ADD 330)   676 BC

House sale: the punishment for any future litigator is to pay 2 minas of silver and 2 minas of gold to Ištar of Arbail and to return the money tenfold to its owners.

SAA 6 214.2   (ADD 40)   676 BC

Loan of 2 talents of copper, first fruits of Ištar of Arbail, belonging to Mannu-ki-Arbail, at the disposal of Šamaš-ahhe-šallim.

SAA 6 219.rev.9   (ADD 1157)   reign of Esarhaddon

Slave sale: the punishment for any future litigator is to pay 1 mina of silver and 1 mina of gold to Ištar of Arbail and to return the money tenfold to its owners.

SAA 6 235.3   (ADD 41)   671 BC

Loan of 1 mina of silver by the mina of Carchemish, first fruits of Ištar of Arbail, belonging to Silim-Aššur, at his disposal.

SAA 6 237.2   (ADD 44)   670 BC

Loan of 12 minas of silver by the mina of Carchemish, first fruits of Ištar of Arbail, belonging to Silim-Aššur, at the disposal of Zarutî son of Gugî.

SAA 6 272.3   (ADD 72)   677 BC

Loan of [x shekels of silver, first fruits of Ištar of Arbail, belonging to] Nusku-naṣir, at the disposal of [PN].

SAA 6 291.2   (ADD 42)   670 BC

Loan of ½ mina of silver, capital of Ištar of Arbail, belonging to Eriba-Adad at the disposal of [...]-ilu.

SAA 7 58 (ADD 1110+) not dated

Issue of [gold] and silver rings, including to the servants who brought the horse teams to Arbail (ii.6); to the emissaries of the lady Yatia when they brought the horses to Arbail (rev.ii.18); and to the emissaries and city rulers who brought the tribute to Arbail (rev. iii.18).

Gold armbands from the royal tombs at Nimrud (Iraq Museum, Baghdad).

SAA 7 150.rev.ii.14 (ADD 834+) not dated

Issues of meat to a scholar (*ummānu*) of Arbail.

SAA 7 151.rev.i.15 (ADD 981) not dated

Issues of meat to a scholar (*ummānu*) of Arbail.

SAA 7 153.rev.ii.5 (ADD 1046) not dated

Issues of meat to a scholar (*ummânu*) of Arbail.

SAA 7 3.i.7 (ADD 853) not dated

Misu, governor of Arbail, listed in lists of governors and high officials.

SAA 7 4.i.9 (ADD 854) not dated

Misu, governor of Arbail, listed in lists of governors and high officials.

SAA 10 6.8 (ABL 386) Esarhaddon

Letter to the king stating that the scribes of Nineveh, Kilizi and Arbail could enter a treaty ceremony (*adê*) while those of Assur have not yet come.

SAA 10 18.rev.8 (ABL 35) Esarhaddon

Letter to the king stating that the *taklimtu* (a display connected with the cult of Dumuzi) should take place in Arbail on the 27th to the 29th of the month.

SAA 10 19.rev.7 (ABL 1097) Esarhaddon

Letter to the king stating that the display (*taklimtu*) should take place in Arbail on the 27th, 28th and 29th of the month.

SAA 10 20.rev.4 (ABL 343) Esarhaddon

Fragmentary letter concerning the arranging of a festival, Arbail mentioned.

SAA 10 96.21 (ABL 43) Esarhaddon/Ashurbanipal

Letter concerning affairs of the Aššur temple in which it is stated that among others the (governor of) Arbail has not sent in the regular delivery of barley and emmer.

SAA 10 136.3 (ABL 982) Esarhaddon/Ashurbanipal

Letter to the crown prince from the foreman of the decury of (scribes) of Arbail; contents damaged.

SAA 10 137.3 (ABL 432) Esarhaddon/Ashurbanipal

Letter to the crown prince from the foreman of the decury of (scribes) of Arbail concerning an eclipse.

SAA 10 138.5 (ABL 423) Esarhaddon/Ashurbanipal

Letter to the crown prince from the foreman of the decury of (scribes) of Arbail reporting that the moon could not be observed due to cloudy conditions.

SAA 10 139.5 (ABL 829) Esarhaddon/Ashurbanipal

Letter to the crown prince from the foreman of the decury of (scribes) of Arbail reporting that the moon could not be observed due to cloudy conditions.

SAA 10 140.4   (HAV 256f)   Esarhaddon/Ashurbanipal

Letter to the crown prince from the foreman of the decury of (scribes) of Arbail reporting that the moon could not be seen on the 29th.

Waxed ivory writing-board, 720–710 BC. One of a set of 16 boards hinged together as a folding set which were intended for the palace of Sargon II at Khorsabad, containing the omen series of Enuna Anu Enlil for interpreting astrological events (British Museum, London - BM 131952).

SAA 10 141.4   (ABL 671)   Esarhaddon/Ashurbanipal

Letter to the crown prince from the foreman of the decury of (scribes) of Arbail reporting that the moon could not be seen on the 29th.

SAA 10 142.4   (ABL 1438)   Esarhaddon/Ashurbanipal

Letter to the crown prince from the foreman of the decury of (scribes) of Arbail reporting that the moon was seen on the 29th.

SAA 10 151.5   (CT 53 915)   Esarhaddon/Ashurbanipal

Letter to the king reporting that the moon was not observed due to cloudy conditions and recommending that messengers are sent to the Inner City of Arbail.

SAA 10 205   (ABL 13)   Esarhaddon/Ashurbanipal

Fragmentary letter concerning offerings for Šatru.

SAA 10 254.4 (ABL 1168) 670 BC[88]

Letter concerning ritual against cultic offences written after the king has made an entry into Arbail.

SAA 10 284.rev.5 (ABL 58) Esarhaddon/Ashurbanipal

Letter to the king recommending that an individual be banished from Assyria, quoting that Ištar of Nineveh and Ištar of Arbail have said "We shall root out from Assyria those who are not loyal to the king our lord".

SAA 10 287.3 (CT 53 929) Esarhaddon/Ashurbanipal

Letter concerning the king's robes in Arbail.

SAA 10 294.rev.14 (ABL 1285) Esarhaddon

Letter from a scholar to the king about grievances and stating he has walked three times to Arbail and once to Aššur (presumably to petition the king).

SAA 10 369.rev.6 (ABL 339) Esarhaddon

Letter to the king complaining that the governor of Dur-Šarrukin has broken the seal of the treasury of the temple of Simalu'a and Humhum, and mentioning that the governors of Nineveh and Arbail have taken silver.

Impression of the royal seal of Sargon II, 715 BC, found at Nineveh. The royal seals have similar designs, but this example is unusual in being named and dated (British Museum, London – SM.2276).

SAA 11 7.2' (K 13076) no date

Fragmentary list of contributions from provinces.

88. SAA 10 p. 201, Parpola 1983 p. 192f.

SAA 11 51.1 (Iraq 27 p. 16 no. 22) 695 BC

Sealing from a shipment of silver to Arbail: "1 talent (of silver) of the orchard of Arbail. Month of Kanun, day 4, eponymy of Aššur-belu-uṣur".

SAA 13 96.14 (ABL 64) 621 BC

Letter from Nabû-šumu-iddina to the king reporting arrivals of consignments of equids, including mules from Kilizi and Arbail.

SAA 13 138.4.10 (ABL 1389) Ashurbanipal

Letter from Aššur-hamatua reporting that Nabû-epuš the priest of Ea has stolen property of Ištar (and) removed the golden [...] from the massive offering table before Ištar.

SAA 13 139.rev.7 (ABL 1249) Ashurbanipal

Letter from Aššur-hamatua reporting an oracular utterance (?).

SAA 13 140 (ABL 1098) Ashurbanipal

Letter from Aššur-hamatua to the king concerning royal images standing on the left and rights side of Ištar (in Arbail).

Statue of Shalmaneser III: statues such as this stood on either side of the cult statue of Ishtar in the Egašankalamma (Istanbul Archaeological Museums).

SAA 13 141   (CT 53 18)   Ashurbanipal

Letter from Aššur-hamatua to the
king reporting that work on statues
for the temple of Ištar (of Arbail)
is completed and that the copper
has been delivered.

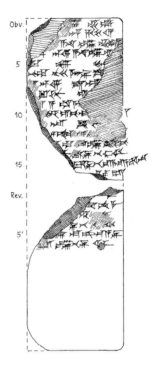

British Museum, London – K 01036

SAA 13 142   (CT 53 223)   Ashurbanipal

Letter from Aššur-hamatua to the king (fragmentary).

SAA 13 143   (ABL 533)   Esarhaddon/Ashurbanipal

Letter to the king from Aplāya the temple steward (*laḫḫinu*) of Ištar of Arbail reporting receipt of a sealed order granting exemption to the servants/slaves (*urdu*) of Ištar.

SAA 13 147.9.11   (ABL 876)   Esarhaddon/Ashurbanipal

Letter to the king reporting that Ištar of Arbail "has gone up to the divine party
(*qarītu*) in Arbail" but that the chief victualler (*rab danibāti*) is refusing to cooperate in
providing sacrificial bread (*liḫmu*).

SAA 13 148.3   (CT 53 413)   Esarhaddon/Ashurbanipal

Letter to the king concerning a female votary (*šēlūtu*) of Ištar of Arbail.

SAA 13 149   (ABL 1164)   670 BC[89]

Letter asking whether the king and Ištar (Šatru) should arrive to meet simultaneously after she comes from Milkia, or whether one of them should be waiting first.

SAA 13 186.rev.10   (SAAB 2 p. 72)   Esarhaddon

Letter from Aplāya the *šangû* of Kurbail concerning the non-delivery of quotas of textiles which in the past were woven by the weavers from Arbail and issued from the palace.

SAA 14 28.2   (ADD 46)   637 BC

Loan of silver, first fruits of Ištar of Arbail, belonging to Kiṣir-Aššur.

SAA 14 36.rev.6   (ADD 446)   630 BC

Sale of a vineyard and two persons: the punishment for any future litigator is to pay 1 mina of silver and 5 minas of gold to Ištar of Arbail and to return the money tenfold to its owners.

SAA 14 108.2   (ADD 1193)   637 BC

Loan of silver of Ištar of Arbail, belonging to Kiṣir-Aššur.

SAA 14 112.rev.5   (ADD 384+)   634 BC

Sale of a field: the punishment for any future litigator is to pay 1 mina of gold to Ištar of Arbail and to return the money tenfold to its owners.

SAA 14 163.4   (ADD 88)   622 BC

Loan of silver of Ištar of Arbail belonging to Nabû-iqbi.

SAA 14 164.1   (ADD 87)   622 BC

Inner tablet to preceding text.

89. For the date see SAA 13 p. 119, note (referring to Parpola 1983, commentaries on LAS No. 192 and 196).

SAA 14 169.2 (ADD 50) 619 BC

Loan of silver, first fruits of Ištar of Arbail belonging to Tuqunu-ereš.

SAA 14 307.rev.3.6 (ADD 587) Late Assyrian

Fragmentary land sale which mentions the governor (^{lú}EN.NAM) and the mayor (^{lú}*ha-za-nu*) of Arbail among the witnesses.

SAA 14 443.rev.12 (TIM 11 14) Late Assyrian

Contract in which the Egyptian Puṭu-eši buys a wife: for as long as Puṭu-eši lives, the woman and her sons will be votaries (*šēlūtu*) of Ištar of Arbail.

SAA 14 466.6 (ADD 485) Late Assyrian

Fragmentary contract in which the punishment for any future litigator is to pay 5 minas of silver and [x] minas of gold to Ištar of Arbail, to tie <4> white horses at the feet of Aššur, to bring four *harbakannu* horses to the feet of Nergal and to return the money tenfold to its owners.

SAA 16 1.10 (ABL 918) Esarhaddon

Letter from Esarhaddon to Urtaku king of Elam, contents mostly broken off, but opening with the statement that "Aššur, Sin, Šamaš, Bel, Nabû, Ištar of Nineveh, Ištar of Arbail and Manziniri have now fulfilled and confirmed what they have promised and have developed our friendship to its peak".

SAA 16 84.rev.9 (ABL 413) Esarhaddon

Letter to the king from Nabû-šarru-uṣur concerning robes for which red wool will be issued to the weavers of Arbail who will come to Kurbail to make them.

SAA 16 93.rev.9 (ABL 1451) Esarhaddon

Letter of which the contents are not entirely clear but which ends with the advice that bodyguards be sent to Assur, Calah, Arbail and Dur-Šarrukin.

SAA 16 120.9 (ABL 143) Esarhaddon
Letter to the king concerning exempt people (${}^{lú}zak$-ku-$ú$) who are outside of Arbail.

SAA 16 121.6 (ABL 333) Esarhaddon
Letter to the king begging mercy for not having arrived on time in Arbail.

SAA 16 123.6.7 (ABL 1343) Esarhaddon
List of personnel of the *rab mūgi*, including two individuals from Arbail.

SAAB 5 p. 47 No. 17 VAT 14450 620 BC
Legal text recording that the (credit for) merchandise (for a business venture) in the mountains (*qiptu ša šadê*) was provided jointly and has been settled: "whoever contravenes (this), may Aššur, Šamaš and Ištar of Arbail be his adversaries in court".

SAAB 5 p. 82 No. 37 VAT 9367 7th century BC
Legal text documenting that a loan of silver has been repaid in full, with a penalty clause stating that if the creditors seek litigation in the future "May Nergal, Aššur, Šamaš, Mullissu, Šerua (and) Ištar of Arbail be their adversaries in court. He will return the sum tenfold to its owner. In his litigation and his lawsuit he will not succeed."

SAAB 5 p. 129 No. 64 VAT 20362 619 BC
Loan of 6½ minas of silver of Ištar of Arbail.

SAAB 9 p. 26 No. 69 VAT 9622 late 7th century BC
Loan of silver of Ištar of Arbail, belonging to Hubašate.

SAAB 9 p. 61 No. 87 VAT 9707 640 BC
Loan of silver of Ištar of Arbail, belonging to Aššur-bessunu.

SAAB 9 p.108 No. 121   VAT 9144   626 BC
Loan of silver, first fruits of Ištar of Arbail, belonging to Mušallim-Aššur.

SAAB 9 p. 109 No. 122   VAT 8766/8787   690 BC
Loan of copper, first fruits of the *qarītu* of Ištar of Arbail, belonging to Nabû'a.

SAAB 9 p. 111 No. 123   VAT 8955   669 BC
Loan of silver, first fruits of Ištar of Arbail, belonging to Tukulti-Aššur.

SAAB 9 p. 119 No. 129   VAT 8936   658 BC
Loan of silver, first fruits of Ištar of Arbail, belonging to Nabû-šar-ahhēšu.

SAAB 9 p. 129 No. 138   VAT 8931   late 7th century BC
Loan of silver, first fruits of Ištar of Arbail, belonging to Nabû-šar-ahhēšu.

StAT 2 No. 4   A 2778.4   692 BC
Loan of silver belonging to Ištar of Arbail.

StAT 2 No. 88   A 1905.2   621 BC
Loan of silver of Ištar of Arbail to two caravan merchants.

StAT 2 No. 164   A 2527.rev.11   675 BC
Contract of marriage of a votaress (*šelūtu*) of Ištar of Arbail whose father was a
horse keeper ([lú]DIB ANŠE.KUR.RA) of Ištar of Arbail.

StAT 2 No. 178   A 0309   629 BC
Slave sale: the punishment for any future litigator is to pay 10 minas of silver and 1
mina of gold to Ištar of Arbail and to return the money tenfold to its owners.

StAT 2 No. 184   A 0310   no date

Contract of marriage of a votaress (*šēlūtu*) of Ištar of Arbail with a curse against any future eunuch, cohort commander or commander of fifty who attempts to seize her.

StAT 2 No. 216   A 1883.2   613 BC

Loan of silver, first fruits of Aššur and Ištar of Arbail.

StAT 2 No. 269   A 1823.rev.5   no date

Slave sale: the punishment for any future litigator is to pay 10 minas of silver and 1 mina of gold to Ištar of Arbail and to return the money tenfold to its owners.

StAT 2 No. 282   A 2640.3   670 BC

Loan of silver belonging to Ištar of Arbail.

StAT 2 No. 288   A 1916.2   624 BC

Loan of silver belonging to Ištar of Arbail.

StAT 2 No. 295   A 3086.2   no date

Loan of silver belonging to Ištar of Arbail.

TCL 9 66.2   AO 4511   no date

Loan of silver of Ištar of Arbail, belonging to Qibit-Aššur.

Other references to **Arbail** in the royal correspondence and administrative material are: Friedrich et al. 1940 p. 29 (Tell Halaf No. 34); Iraq 25 p. 94 (BT 116); KAV 133; SAA 1 127.rev.3; SAA 3 36.9 (fragmentary mythological ritual), 49.3, SAA 5 136.9 (itinerary), 141.rev.5, 150.rev.17; SAA 6 4.2; SAA 8 558.rev.1 (astrological report); SAA 11 7.2, 10.5 (lists of contributions from provinces), SAA 14 265.9, 298.1, 425.rev.24 (a citizen of Arbail among the witnesses to a land sale); SAA 16 122. rev.13; ND 2462 (CTN V p.197), ND 2675 (CTN V p. 287); CT 54 311 rev.7. The **Egašankalamma** is also mentioned in SAA 3 (ABL 1462). **Milkia** is also referred to in SAA 1 125.4 (ABL 191), 146.4 (ABL 136) and 147.4 (ABL 526). Other texts written in Arbail are SAA 6 114.rev.2 and 115.rev.5.

Oracular Pronouncements and Divination

Oracular Pronouncements

SAA 9 1   (4 R2 61)   reign of Esarhaddon

A collection of oracular prophesies to Esarhaddon. Ten prophesies are preserved.
To give the flavour of these prophesies we give the translation of the first one in full;
the translations and interpretations of these texts follow Parpola.

> Esarhaddon king of Assyria, fear not! What wind has risen against you whose wings
> I have not broken? Your enemies will roll before you like ripe apples. I am the Great
> Lady: I am Ištar of Arbail who cast your enemies before your feet. What words have I
> spoken to you that you cannot rely upon? I am Ištar of Arbail. I will flay your enemies
> and give them to you. I am Ištar of Arbail. I will go before you and behind you. Fear
> not! You are paralysed but in the midst of woe I will rise and sit down (beside you).

From the mouth of Issar-la-tašiyat of Arbail.

The sibyls and prophesies of the other pronouncements are as follows:

(2)   Sinqisa-amur: promise to Esarhaddon to keep him safe: "Have no fear ... I will
       keep you safe and defeat your enemies."

(3)   Remutti-allati: "I rejoice with Esarhaddon my king! Arbail rejoices!"

(4)   Bayâ: encouragement to Esarhaddon to put his faith in Ištar of Arbail, who
       also identifies herself as Bel and Nabû.

(5)   Ilussu-amur: text too fragmentary for translation.

(6)   [......]: promise to give Esarhaddon long life, to "take him safely across the
       river", to defeat his enemies.

(7)   Issar-beli-da"ini: promise to destroy [his enemies].

(8)   Ahat-abiša: prophesy to the Queen Mother "Fear not, my king: the kingship is
       yours! Power is yours!"

(9)   [......]: assurance that "All is well with Esarhaddon, king of Assyria: Ištar has gone out to the steppe and sent (an oracle of) well being to her calf in the city."

(10)   La-dagil-ili: encouragement to Esarhaddon to praise Ištar and promise that "You shall eat safe food and drink safe water and you will be safe in your palace. Your son and grandson shall rule as kings on the lap of Ninurta."

SAA 9 2   (TI Pl.2f+)   reign of Esarhaddon
A collection of oracular prophesies to Esarhaddon of which six are preserved in whole or in part. The sibyls and prophesies of these pronouncements are as follows:

(1)   Nabû-hassanni: promise to destroy the enemies of Esarhaddon.

(2)   Bayâ: promise to defeat the enemies of Esarhaddon, protect him and give him long life.

(3)   La-dagil-ili: promise to destroy the enemies of Esarhaddon, to bring about stability in Assyria, to keep him safe and that his son and grandson will rule in Assyria.

(4)   Urkittu-šarrat: promise to Esarhaddon to search out for traitors ... and to choose the emissaries of the Elamite and Mannean (kings), to seal the writings of the Urartian (king) and to cut off the [...] of Mugallu.

(5)   Sinqisa-amur: encouragement to Esarhaddon not to be afraid: "I will protect my king. I will bring his enemies in neckstocks and vassals with tribute before his feet."

(6)   [......]: encouragement [to Esarhaddon] not to be afraid.

SAA 9 3   (ABRT 1, 22f)   reign of Esarhaddon

The "Covenant of Aššur" - an oracular prophesy made to Esarhaddon by the prophetess La-dagil-ili. There are five sections: (1) introduction; (2) "First Oracle of Salvation" in which it is prophesied that the king will vanquish his enemies (Melid, the Cimmerians and the land of Ellipi are mentioned specifically) and that Aššur has given him rule over the whole world; (3) "Second Oracle of Salvation" which recounts that Aššur has banished and slaughtered the traitors who surrounded Esarhaddon; (4) "Meal of the Covenant" which opens with "The word of Ištar to Esarhaddon king of Assyria" and recounts the vision of the prophet that Ištar gathered together the gods, gave them food and water and enjoined them to repeat the ceremony in their own cities in order to remember the covenant; (5) a second "Word of Ištar to Esarhaddon king of Assyria" which recapitulates the above.

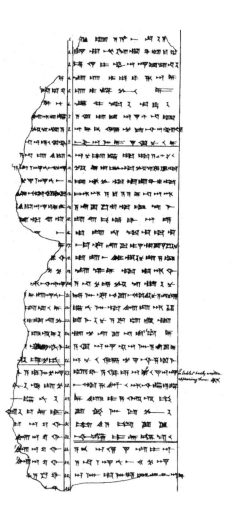

British Museum, London – K 02401.

SAA 9 4   (83-1-18, 839)   reign of Esarhaddon

Fragment of a collection of oracles of encouragement to Esarhaddon, king of Assyria.

SAA 9 5   (TI 4l.4)   reign of Esarhaddon

Oracular report of the word of Ištar of Arbail (*a-bat* ᵈ15) to the Queen Mother that the king will be safe and his enemies will be defeated.

SAA 9 6   (Bu 91-5-9, 106+)   reign of Esarhaddon

Report of an oracle uttered by Tašmetu-ereš in Arbail that Ištar of Arbail will bring order to Assyria and defeat the enemies of the king.

SAA 9 7   (ABRT 1, 26f)   reign of Esarhaddon

Prophesy uttered by Mullissu-kabtat that Ištar of Arbail will protect Ashurbanipal (while crown prince), that he will be safe and that he will come to rule Assyria and the world.

SAA 9 9   (ABL 1280)   reign of Ashurbanipal

Report to Ashurbanipal of an oracle made by Dunnaša-amur of Arbail that Ištar of Arbail is devoting all her energies to ensuring the life of Ashurbanipal and that his enemies will be defeated. "I have ordained life for you in the assembly of all the gods ... I keep demanding life for you!"

SAA 9 10   (CT 53 946)   reign of Ashurbanipal

Fragment of a report to Ashurbanipal of an oracle made by Dunnaša-amur that [Ištar] will give him kingship and long life.

SAA 9 11   (CT 53 219)   Ashurbanipal

Fragment of a report to Ashurbanipal of an oracle that [Ištar] will defeat his enemies and restore order to the land.

SAA 4 300   (PRT 135)   reign of Ashurbanipal

Text recording an oracular question asking whether Ashurbanipal should appoint Sin-tabni-uṣur as governor of Ur. Performed in Arbail.

SAA 4 195   (PRT 50)   reign of Esarhaddon

Text recording an oracular question put to Šamaš concerning whether a woman (whose name is missing) will be struck by the disease "hand of a ....". Performed in Arbail.

SAA 4 324   (PRT 110)   651 BC

Report on an extispiscy. The preserved quotations of apodoses from omen collections deal with the enemy being defeated or not achieving his ambition and that the "prince's country will expand". Performed in Arbail.

Hymns and Ritual texts

A number of tablets are known with compositions which might broadly be called literary and which relate to the cult of Ištar/Šatru. These include a hymn of Shalmaneser, two hymns of Ashurbanipal and a cultic commentary.

Shalmaneser's Hymn to Ištar of Arbail
(KAR 98)[90]

This composition is preserved on a tablet from Assur. The beginning and end are unfortunately missing; the preserved sections gives the titles of Shalmaneser followed by an account of his restoration of the temple harp[91] and of a statue.[92] A joyful entry into Milkia is also mentioned.

90. Meinhold 2009 pp. 291–300. Although KAR 98 was published in 1919, remarkably until Meinhold's edition there was no published treatment of the text; cf. Foster 2005 pp. 782–3.

91. It is not completely certain that the object in question was a harp. The word used is *tibu'u* (spelled *ti-bi-'u*) and while both dictionaries agree in taking this as a form of *timbuttu* "harp" they do not justify this identification.

92. The identification of the second object of Shalmaneser's attention is also not certain. The text has *si pi ir nu*, which could be read either as a singular noun *si-pi-ir-nu* or as *si-pi-ir* NU the "*sipru* of the statue" (NU then being a logogram for *ṣalmu* "statue"). In either case the meaning is unclear: a word *sipirnu* is not otherwise attested and while a word *sipru* "rubble" is documented, a restoration of the rubble of the statue would be unusual if not impossible.

[.......... Shalmaneser ......] foremost prince, warrior, favourite of the able goddess, trusted prefect, beloved of Ištar, who grasps your hem, beseeched your divinity: "O Lady you have searched him out, you have desired his lordship over (all) the kings of the world. You have made his kingship splendid. The kings whom with their royal headdresses you have entrusted into his hands are gathered bowed before him (and) kiss his feet." Faithful shepherd, provider of the shrines, son of Ashurnasirpal, priest of Aššur, [king of Assyria], descendant of Tukulti-Nin[urta, likewise priest of Aššur], who provides your *serqu*-offerings and presents your *nindabû*-offerings, faithful shepherd, appointee of Aššur whom [your hands cre]ated, majestic, who goes before [you], who performed your rites.

   The great harp which sung (of) your divinity had become old and I made a harp for songs of jubilation. I renewed, embellished and increased its fittings and made them better than before. I fixed a star of shining amber resting on (its) top. Bowing I prayed to your lordly image, "O Mullissu, in your grace give him life! (This is) the harp and drum, beloved to you, which makes your heart glad (and) brightens your spirit". I restored the ... of the statue. I decorated its base with a mountain goat, an ass (and) animals of the high mountains of copper (and) hard wood. They fitted rings of shining gold as its handles. [With] joy [I entered] into Milkia [and performed] the ceremony of the Queen. The Lady of Arbail [.......]

In all probability the harp was restored and the hymn composed as part of the victory celebrations held in Arbail at the conclusion of Shalmaneser's campaign against Urartu.

The harp in the Egašankalama was evidently a magnificent instrument. The reconstruction of the much earlier harp from Ur provides some indication of the lavish decoration which these early Mesopotamian musical instruments could receive.

Ashurbanipal's Hymn to Erbil
(SAA 3 8 = LKA 32)[93]

The Hymn to Erbil is inscribed on a tablet in Istanbul Archaeological Museums

1 Arbail, O Arbail!
2 Heaven without equal, O Arbail!
3 City of pleasure, Arbail!
4 City of festivals, Arbail!
5 City of the house of rejoicings, Arbail!
6 Shrine of Arbail, lofty hostel,
7 Spacious Ekurra, sanctuary of delights!
8 Gate of Arbail, pinnacle of holy towns!
9 City of statues, Arbail!
10 Abode of jubilation, Arbail!
11 Arbail! Home of reason and counsel,
12 Bond of the lands, Arbail!
13 Establisher of profound rights, Arbail!
14 Arbail is as lofty as heaven,
15 Its foundations are as secure as the firmaments.
16 The prominences of Arbail are lofty, they rival [.......]
17 Its likeness is Babylon, its rival is Assur.

93. Ebeling 1952, Livingstone 1989 No. 8; the translation follows Livingstone.

18 Lofty sanctuary, shrine of fates, gate of heaven!
19 Tribute enters into it from all the world.
20 Ištar dwells there, (and) Nanaya daughter of Sin [...],
21 Irnina,⁹⁴ foremost of the gods, firstborn goddess.
22 City of consent, city of the consent of Nanaya, this abode!
23 [......] Arbail in all [......]
24 [Among all] the lands does not rival [......]
25 [......] temple of jubilation
26 [......] purify and [......]
27 [......] Egašankalamma [......]
28 [......] like [......]

(*break*)

31 [......] lofty [......]
[......] temple and city [......]
33 [......] play [......]

reverse
1 [......] like [......]
2 All lands rejoice [......]
3 Those who depart from Arbail and those who enter it
4 Are glad, they rejoice and [......].
5 The divine lady is seated on a lion; on a [......];
6 Mighty lions crouch below her,
7 Kings of (all) land(s) are cowered before her.
8 [She holds] domination over beasts.
9 All sacrifices [*are made*] for the well being of the body,
10 All flour offerings [*are made*] for the well being of the body,
11 [The ...... (of)] the courtyard [of] shining Arbail is put in place.
12 The *pigû* drum of the [......] is tuned,
13 The lyre of the [......] is tuned,
14 The [......] of the *kurgarrû* (a cultic performer) is tuned,
15 The [......] is tuned to the songs of the hierodules,
16 The *dubdubbu* drum is tuned, the [.......] of the kettledrums.
17 Glad is the heart [......] under the pra[ise of the ......].
18 Arbail rejoices, the people rejoice,
19 The Lady rejoices, [...... rejoices],
20 The house of [.....] rejoices.
21 The temple is adorned with sumptuousness [......]
22 The Lady of the temple of Arbail rejoices, her heart [......]
23 The advances of [the .....] are lengthened by her merrymaking.
24 [......] Arbail [......]
25 [May] your city [......], may it rule [forever]!

94. line 21 Irnina: according to Gelb (1960 pp. 78–79), Irnina was originally a river goddess with connections to the underworld later subsumed into the identity of Innina and then Ištar.

Ashurbanipal's Hymn to the Ištars of Nineveh and Arbail
(SAA 3 3)[95]

Exalt and Glorify the Lady of Nineveh, magnify and praise the Lady of Arbail, who have no equal among the great gods! Their names are most precious among the goddesses! Their cult centres have no equal among the shrines! A word from their lips is blazing fire! Their utterances are valid forever! I am Ashurbanipal, their favourite, most valued seed of Aššur, offspring of Nineveh, product of the Emašmaš and the Egašankalamma, whose kingship they made great even in the House of Succession. In their pure mouths is voiced the endurance of my throne. I knew no father or mother, I grew up in the lap of my goddesses. As a child the great gods guided me, going with me on the right and the left. They established at my side a good genie and a good angel, assigned my life to guardians of well-being and health. They glorified my stature and fortified my strength; they spread my fame over all rulers. [All enemies] heard (of me) [all] the recalcitrant lands which had not submitted to the kings my fathers and had not brought [tribute and] gifts before them trembled with fear. I am Ashurbanipal, the creation of the hands of the great gods. [.....] goddesses [......] greatly
(*break*)
[......] their command [......] their words. Not [with] my [own strength], not with the strength of my bow, but with the power [and] strength of my goddesses, I made the lands disobedient to me submit to the yoke of Aššur. Unceasingly, yearly they bring me [sumptuous] presents and protect daily the gate of Aššur and Mullissu. They seek peace with me in prayer and in supplication; with observance and prayer they kiss my feet.

As for me, Ashurbanipal, scion of kingship, who slays the recalcitrant and calms the heart of the gods, the great gods gave me confidence and blessed my weapons, the Lady of Nineveh, the mother who bore me, endowed me with unparalleled kingship; the Lady of Arbail, my creator, ordered everlasting life (for me). They decreed as my fate to exercise dominion over all inhabited regions and made their kings bow down at my feet. May the Lady of Nineveh, lady of song, magnify my kingship forever!

95. OECT 6 11. The translation follows Livingstone SAA 3 3.

Prayer to Ishtar of Arbail
Lambert 2006 p.38

A prayer to Ištar of Arbail appears together with a prayer to Ištar of Nineveh in a Neo-Assyrian ritual text reconstructed by Lambert from the fragments of cuneiform tablets of at least four copies:

> [Ištar], great [lady] who dwells in the Egašankalamma,
> [Lady] of Arbail, most noble of goddesses,
> [... of] heaven and earth, giver of life,
> [...] lion, able, Ištar
> [...] whose command cannot be altered,
> The command of her heart [cannot] be changed,
> No god can understand [her ...],
> Ištar, great lady who dwells in the Egašankalamma.
> At this offering etc.

Prayer to Ištar of Arbail

The penultimate line here refers to ritual protocols which will have been stipulated in full earlier.

Commentary on rites in Egašankalamma
(TIM 9 59 = SAA 3 38)

Cultic commentary beginning with the rubric "[The rites which] are performed in the Egašankalamma are [enacted] like those of Nippur" and giving mythological explanations for acts in the cult.

KAR 215/STT 88[94]
Another reference to cultic practice is to be found in a text dealing with ritual instructions:

ki-i ina ᵘʳᵘ4-DINGIR *ina* IGI ᵈ15 MUN MIN *Aš+šur* ᵈ15 TI.LA *mu-uh-ru ta-qab-bi*

If you strew salt before Ištar in Arbail, you should say "Aššur, Ištar: receive life!"

---

94. Ebeling PKTA 10f; Or 21 pp. 129–135.

Ištar of Arbail

The special place held by Ištar of Arbail both in Arbail and within Assyria as a whole will be clear from many of the entries above.[97] Further indications of the goddess' importance are to be found from her appearance among the deities invoked in royal inscriptions, her presence among the deities witnessing treaties and her inclusion in the greeting formulae of letters.

Royal inscriptions

Starting at least with Sennacherib, royal inscriptions list Ištar of Arbail among the deities supporting the kings in their campaigns. Ištar of Arbail appears in this capacity alongside Aššur, Ninlil, Ningal, Šerua, Sin, Marduk, Bel, Nabû, Nergal, Šamaš, Adad, Ištar of Nineveh, Šarrat Kidmuri, Gula, Anu, Enlil, and the Sibitti.

Treaties

In treaties Ištar of Arbail is mentioned as one of the deities by which the parties swear and who will administer punishment upon the contravenor.[98] The other deities mentioned alongside include (not exhaustively) Aššur, Mullissu, Šerua, Sin, Nikkal, Šamaš, Nur, Anu, Antu, Illil, Adad, Šala, Kippat-mati, Ištar of Heaven, Ištar of Nineveh, the Assyrian Ištar, Zababa, Babu, Nabû, Uraš and Ninurta, Nusku, Marduk, Ea, Belet-ili, Kakka and Nergal, and the gods of the Akītu chapel. In some cases we have the exact punishment allocated to the role of the goddess:

> May Ištar who dwells in Arbail not show you mercy and compassion

SAA 2, 5.iv.2   [Esarhaddon's treaty with Baal, king of Tyre]
SAA 2, 6.459   [Vassal Treaty of Esarhaddon]

> May Ištar who resides in Arbail, goddess of battle, [break our bows in the thick of battle and] make us crouch [under the feet of] our enemy

---

97. An earlier review of the evidence for the cult in Arbail can be found in Menzel 1981 pp. 6–11; note that "Arbail along with Mullissu" appears among the cult cities listed in the literary text edited by George, SAAB 1 (1987) p. 31f.

98. SAA 2 2.vi.16, 3.9.rev.4, 6.20, 10.rev.10.

The goddess is similarly invoked in the formula of curses against anyone who destroys literary tablets.[99]

Letter formulae

Ištar of Arbail also appears in the greetings formulae of letters to the king from Assyrian scholars along with Aššur, Bel, Nabû, Sin, Nergal, Marduk, Ištar of Nineveh, Mullissu, the Lady of Kidmuri, Adad, Šala, Nikkal, Šamaš, Gula, Ninurta, Laṣ, Ṣarpanitu, and the planets Mercury, Venus, Jupiter and Saturn.[100] And throughout the inscriptions of Esarhaddon and Ashurbanipal Ištar of Erbil is listed as one of the deities who supports the king on campaign.[101]

Other references to Ištar of Arbail are KAV 174.rev.3 (order to supply a bird for offerings); SAA 4 316.rev.2 (a pot of Ištar of Arbail appears in a dream) and SAA 14 211.5, 265.rev.3 (penalty clause).

Incidentally, Ištar was not the only deity worshipped in Erbil, as evidenced by the invocation of "all the gods of Arbail" in the Vassal Treaty of Esarhaddon (along with all the gods of the Inner City (Assur), Nineveh, Calah, Kilizi and Harran, as well as all the gods of Babylon, Borsippa and Nippur; indeed all the gods of Assyria and of Sumer and Akkad). Note also the invocation "May the gods who dwell in Arbail bless the king my lord" in SAA 13 140.rev.3.

99. SAA 3 35.70.

100. SAA 10 82.7, 83.5, 130.7, 140.8, 141.8, 142.8, 174.6.19, 197.12, 227.5, 228.5, 233.5, 245.6, 248.7, 249.3, 252.8, 253.8, 286.6, 293.4, 294.3, 345.8; SAA 13 8.8, 9.8, 10.8, 12.6, 13.8, 14.7, 15.8, 56.6, 57.8, 58.7, 60.6, 61.7, 62.7, 64.7, 65.7, 66.6, 67.6, 68.6, 140.7, 143.4, 156.7, 187.rev.6; SAA 16 33.7, 49.5, 59.3, 60.3, 61.3, 106.7, 126.6, 127.6, 128.5.

101. e.g. Borger 1956 Ass D 3; Nin A I 6.10.45.59, II 46, IV 79, V 34, VI 44; Nin B I 7; Nin C II 5; Trb A 26; AsBbA 2.

Personal names

The name of the city appears in the male names Arbail-ilā'ī, Arbail-šumu-iddin, Mannu-ki-Arbail and the hypocoristic Arbailāyu; and in the female names Arbailītu-bēltūni, Arbailtu-bēltu-taqqini, Arbail-hammat, Arbail-lāmur, Arbail-šarrat, Arbailītu and Arbailtu. The following is a single example:

SAA 14 20   K 309a   636 B.C.
Contract for the purchase by Kiṣir-Aššur of slave-woman Arbail-šarrat.

British Museum, London – K 309a

Neo-Babylonian and Achaemenid Sources

In 612 BC Nineveh was sacked by a coalition of the Babylonians and the Medes (supported by the Cimmerians). Elements of the Assyrian aristocracy fell back on Harran but by 605 BC at the latest the Assyrian Empire had come to an end. Its territory was divided between the Medes who took the mountainous areas east of Assyria and probably the northern part of Assyria proper, and the Babylonians who had regained control of Babylonia and took over Assyria up to the city of Assur as well as Transpotamia and the Levant.[102] This paved the way for the Neo-Babylonian Empire. Unfortunately no texts are at present known referring to Erbil from this period other than a solitary reference in the Neo-Babylonian Chronicle. It is probable that at the partition of Assyria Erbil fell to the share of the Medes though this is not known for certain, nor is it known whether at some later stage the city subsequently came under Babylonian rule.

The Babylonian empire lasted until 639 BC, when Cyrus invaded Babylonia, defeated the last native Babylonian king Nabonidus and laid the foundations for the Achaemenid Empire. This proved to be a period of great growth and stability, lasting until 331 BC when Alexander in his turn invaded, defeated Darius III and brought that empire to an end, events referred to in an astronomical diary. Sources referring to Erbil during this period are limited. Nevertheless the combination of archaeological data and references from classical sources indicate that it must have been a prospering city of major importance.[103]

Historical texts

Neo-Babylonian Chronicle
According to the Neo-Babylonian Chronicle, in the ninth year of Nabonidus (547 BC) Cyrus crossed with his army below Erbil (*šaplan* uru*Arbail*) when he marched through Assyria on his way to the west.[104]

British Museum, London – BM 35382

102. MacGinnis 2010.

103. Kuhrt 1990 p. 185–186.

104. Grayson 1975a p. 107 Chronicle VII.ii.16; Glassner 2005 p. 236 l.16; for the interpretation that this campaign of Cyrus' was against Urartu, and not as had long been imagined against Croesus of Lydia, see Rollinger 2008.

Behistun

In the inscription on the cliff face of Behistun (Bisitun), Darius describes how he despatched his general Takhmaspada at the head of an army of Persian and Median troops to defeat the Sagartian rebel Shitrantakhma (Tritantaechmes) who had risen up claiming to be a descendant of Cyaxares.[105] The Babylonian and Old Persian versions give the same details of what followed:

Shitrantakhma, the rebel leader impaled at Erbil, is centre in the line of 9 bound prisoners; he claimed descent from Median royalty.

> Under the protection of Ahura Mazda my troops defeated the rebels. On the 5th day of Tašritu they fought the battle. They captured Shitrantakhma and sent him to me. Then I cut off his nose, his two ears, his tongue (and) blinded him in one eye, He was held in fetters at my gate. All the people could see him. Then I impaled him in Arbail. The total dead and surviving of the rebel force was 447.

The Behistun text was widely circulated elsewhere in the Achaemenid empire, written on other materials, as in the case of this Aramaic version, on papyrus, from Elephantine in Egypt (Neues Museum, Berlin – Papyrus 13447).

105. Voigtlander 1978 p. 53 II 33.66, 23.63, 90; OP Paragraph 33, Babylonian Section 26.

Administrative texts

Babylonian

BM 62805   MacGinnis 2004 p.32   reign of Cyrus

Administrative text from the Ebabbara, the temple of Šamaš in Sippar, dating to the reign of Cyrus recording "10 bronze rings of the Lady of Arbail ... brought into the *bīt karê* (a storehouse of the Ebabbara)"

Elamite

There are a number of unpublished texts from the Persepolis Fortification Archive (which spans 509–495 BC) mentioning a location by the name of [BEH]*ar-be-ra-an* which may be a writing of Erbil. The *Répertoire Géographique* (Vallat 1993 p. 83) lists the following:

PF-NN 1001.4 (Fort 3847)
PF-NN 1739.4 (Fort 6685)
PF-NN 2342.27 (Fort 9017)

There will almost certainly be further additions to this list. However no further information on the contents of these texts is available at present.

Passport of Nehtihur

Letter of Arsames written for Nehtihur, ordering the officers in charge of the provinces through which he will pass on his way to Egypt to provide him with rations.[106] The rations are to be taken from Arsames' estates in these provinces and are to consist of flour, wine or beer, and sheep for the men (ten retainers of Nehtihur plus two Cilicians and one craftsman) and hay for the horses. Erbil (*'rbl*) is listed as one of these stations. The letter dates to the late 5th century BC. A possible reconstruction of the route taken by Nehtihur is shown on the map on page 38.

The passport of Nehtihur is written in Aramaic on leather. It was found among a collection of letters in Egypt, where Arsames was satrap (Bodleian Library, Oxford – Pell. Aram. VIII int.).

106.   Driver 1954 p.27–28 No.6.

Astronomical Diary

BM 36390+36761   Sachs & Hunger 1988 p. 179, No. -330   331 BC

Fragmentary astronomical diary for months V and VI of the fifth year of Darius III including the entry (obv.15'–18'):

> On the 24th (i.e. October 1st, 331 BC) the king of the world (i.e. Darius) [planted] his standard [......] they fought opposite each other and (Alexander) [inflicted a heavy defeat on the troops [of the king ......] the king. His troops deserted him and [fled] to their cities [......] they fled [to the] land of Gutium (i.e. into the Zagros)

After some data on astronomical observations and commodity prices the diary gives details on communications in which Alexander assures the Babylonians that the temple of Esagila will be restored and orders them to remain in their houses. A part of the Greek army precedes Alexander into Esagila, sacrifices are made and then comes the historic line (rev.11')

> Alexander, the king of the world, entered Babylon

The tablet describes the omens before the battle, which included a lunar eclipse on 20 September 331 BC one hour and 10 minutes after sunset, while Saturn was present and Jupiter had set shortly before the eclipse was complete. A lunar eclipse while Jupiter was invisible was considered a bad omen for the reigning Persian king, and was interpreted by the Macedonians as favourable to themselves (British Museum, London – BM 36761).

Bibliography

Abdul-Hadi al Fouadi 1978: "Inscriptions and reliefs from Bitwāta" (*Sumer* 34, 122–129).

Albenda P 1980: "An unpublished drawing of Louvre AO 19914 in the British Museum", *JTS* 12, 1–8.

Ali Yaseen Ahmed 1996: "The Archive of Aššur-mātu-taqqin found in the New Town of Aššur and dated mainly by post-canonical eponyms" (*Al-Rafidain* 17, 207–288).

Andrae W 1923: *Farbige Keramik aus Assur und ihre Vorstufen in altassyrischen Wandmalereien.* Berlin.

Archi A & G Biga 2003: "A Victory over Mari and the Fall of Ebla" (*JCS* 55, 1–44).

Ardalan O Hassan 2008: "Three Inscriptions in Betwata" (*Subartu* 2, 10–17) [in Kurdish].

Astour M C 1987: "Semites and Hurrians in northern Transtigris" in M A Morrison & D I Owen (eds) *Studies on the civilization and culture of Nuzi and the Hurrians, 2, general studies and excavations at Nuzi 9/11: in honor of Ernest R. Lacheman on his seventyfifth birthday, April 29 1981* (Winona Lake), 3–68.

Ayish A H 1976: "Bassetki Statue with an Old Akkadian Inscription of Naram-Sin of Agade (B.C. 2291–2255)" (*Sumer* 32, 63–75).

Bauer T 1933: *Das Inschriftwerk Assurbanipals* I–II. Leipzig.

Borger R 1956: *Die Inschriften Asarhaddons Königs von Assyrien* (*AfO* Beiheft 9).

Graz 1996: *Beiträge zum Inschriftenwerk Assurbanipals.* Wiesbaden.

Brinkman J A 1968: *A Political History of Post-Kassite Babylonia.* Rome.

——1982: "Babylonia, c. 1000–748 BC" (*CAH* III/1, 281–311).

——1984: *Prelude to Empire – Babylonian Society and Politics, 747–626 B.C.* Philadelphia.

Charpin D 2004: "Chroniques bibliographiques 3. Données nouvelles sur la région du Petit Zab au XVIIIe siècle" (*RA* 98, 151–178).

Charpin D, O Edzard & M Stol 2004: *Mesopotamien. Die altbabylonische Zeit.* Orbis Biblicus et Orientalis 160/4. Göttingen.

Charpin D & N Ziegler 2003: *Mari et le Proche-Orient à l'époque amorrite. Essai d'histoire politique* (Florilegium Marianum 5). Paris.

Chavalas M W 2006: *The Ancient Near East: historical sources in translation.* Oxford: Blackwells, 98–102.

Colliva L, A Colucci & G F Guidi 2011: "Geophysical prospections with GPR RIS/MF System: a Preliminary Archaeological Survey on Erbil Citadel", in *Preservation of Cultural Heritage of the Kurdistan Region of Iraq. Italian Cooperation Project in Iraqi Kurdistan (2009–2010)*, C G Careti & R Giunta (eds). ISIAO. Rome.

Cohen M E 1993: *The Cultic Calendars of the Ancient Near East.* Bethesda.

Curtis J E 2003: "The Assyrian heartland in the period 612–539 BC", in G Lanfranchi et al. (eds) *Continuity of Empire.* Padova, 157–167.

Dalley S 1993: "Nineveh after 612 BC" (*Altorientalische Forschungen* 20, 134–147).

Dandamayev M A 1997 : "Assyrian Traditions during Achaemenid Times" in S Parpola and R M Whiting (eds) *Assyria 1995* (Helsinki).

Deller K-H 1984: "Drei wiederentdeckte neuassyrische Rechtsurkunden aus Aššur" (*BaM* 15, 225–252).

——1990: "Eine Erwägung zur Lokalisierung des aB ON Qabrā/Qabarā" (*NABU* 1990/3 No. 84).

Deszo T 2006: "Reconstruction of the Assyrian Army of Sargon II (721–705 BC) based on Nimrud Horse Lists" (*SAAB* 15, 93–140).

Donbaz V 1976: *Ninurta-tukulti-Assur. Zamanina ait orta Asur Idarî belgeleri.* Ankara.

Donbaz V & G Frame 1983: "The Building Activities of Shalmaneser I in Northern Mesopotamia" (*Annual Review of the Royal Inscriptions of Mesopotamia Project* 1, 1–5).

Donbaz V & A Harrak 1989: "The Middle Assyrian Eponymy of Kidin-Aššur" (*JCS* 41, 217–225).

Donbaz V & S Parpola 2001: Neo-Assyrian Legal Texts in Istanbul (*Studien zu den Assur-Texten* 2). Saarbrücken.

Driver G R 1954: *Aramaic Documents of the Fifth century B.C.* Oxford.

Ebeling E 1952: "Ein Preislied auf die Kultstadt Arba-ilu aus neuassyrischer Zeit" (*Jahrbuch für kleinasiatische Forschung* 2, 274–282).

Eidem J 1992: *The Shemshara Archives 2: The Administrative Texts*. Copenhagen.

Eidem J & J Laessoe 2001: *The Shemshara Archives 1: The Letters*. Copenhagen.

Foster B R 2005: *Before the Muses: An Anthology of Akkadian Literature* (3rd Edition). Bethesda.

Frahm E 1997: *Einleitung in die Sanherib-Inschriften* (*AfO Beiheft* 26). Vienna.

——2002: "Assur 2001: Die Schriftfunde" (*MDOG* 134, 47–86).

Frankfort H, S Lloyd & T Jacobsen 1949: *The Gimilsin Temple and the Palace of the Rulers at Tell Asmar* (OIP 43). Chicago.

Frayne D R 1990: *Old Babylonian Period (2003–1595 BC)* (Royal Inscriptions of Mesopotamia, Early Periods, volume 1). Toronto.

——1993: *Sargonic and Gutian Periods (2334–2113 BC)* (Royal Inscriptions of Mesopotamia Early Periods Volume 2). Toronto.

——1997: *Ur III Period (2112–2004 BC)* (Royal Inscriptions of Mesopotamia Early Periods Volume 3/2). Toronto.

Freydank H 1976: *Mittelassyrische Rechtsurkunden und Verwaltungstexte I*. VS 19. Berlin.

——1982: *Mittelassyrische Rechtsurkunden und Verwaltungstexte II*. VS 21. Berlin.

——1991: *Beiträge zur mittelassyrischen Chronologie und Geschichte. Schriften zur Geschichte und Kultur des Alten Orients* 21. Berlin.

——1994: *Mittelassyrische Rechtsurkunden und Verwaltungstexte III*. WVDOG 92. Berlin.

——1997: "Mittelassyrische Opferlisten aus Assur" in: H Waetzoldt & H Hauptmann (eds), *CRRAI* 39, *HSAO* 6, 47–52.

——2001: *Mittelassyrische Rechtsurkunden und Verwaltungstexte IV*. WVDOG 99. Saarbrücken.

——2004: *Mittelassyrische Rechtsurkunden und Verwaltungstexte V*. WVDOG 106. Saarbrücken.

——2005: *Mittelassyrische Rechtsurkunden und Verwaltungstexte VI*. WVDOG 109. Saarwellingen.

——2006: *Mittelassyrische Rechtsurkunden und Verwaltungstexte VII*. WVDOG 111. Saarwellingen. Friedrich J, G R Meyer, A Ungnad & E F Weidner

——1940 : *Die Inschriften vom Tell Halaf. (Archiv für Orientforschung,* Beiheft 6). Berlin.

Gasche H, J A Armstrong, S W Cole & V G Gurzadyan 1998: *Dating the Fall of Babylon: A Reappraisal of Second-Millennium Chronology*. Ghent.

Gelb I J 1960: "The name of the goddess Innin" (*JNES* 19, 72–79).

Gerardi P 1988: "Epigraphs and Assyrian Palace reliefs: The Development of the Epigraphic Text" (*JCS* 40, 1–35).

Glassner J-J 1993: *Chroniques mésopotamiennes*. Paris.

Grayson A K 1975a: *Assyrian and Babylonian Chronicles (Texts from Cuneiform Sources* 5). Toronto.

——1975b: *Babylonian Historical-Literary Texts*. Toronto.

——1987: *Assyrian Rulers of the Third and Second Millennia BC (to 1115 BC)* (Royal Inscriptions of Mesopotamia Assyrian Periods, volume 1). Toronto.

——1991: *Assyrian Rulers of the Early First Millennia BC I (1114–859 BC)* (Royal Inscriptions of Mesopotamia Assyrian Periods Volume 2). Toronto.

——1996: *Assyrian Rulers of the Early First Millennia BC II (858–745 BC)* (Royal Inscriptions of Mesopotamia Assyrian Periods Volume 3). Toronto.

Hallo W W 1938: "Gutium" (*Reallexikon der Assyriologie* Band 3 p708–719). Berlin and Leipzig.

Heuzey M 1891: *Les Origines Orientales de l'Art*. Paris.

Ismail B K & A Cavigneaux 2003: "Dādušas Siegesstele IM 95200 aus Ešnunna. Die Inschrift" (*BaM* 34, 129–156).

Jacobsen T 1940: "Historical Data" in Frankfort H, S Lloyd & T Jacobsen *The Gimilsin Temple and the Palace of the Rulers at Tell Asmar* (OIP 43) (Chicago), 116–200.

Kärki I 1986: *Die Königsinschriften der dritten Dynastie von Ur*. Studia Orientalia 58. Helsinki.

Kühne H 2002: "Thoughts about Assyria after 612 BC", in L al-Gailani-Werr et al. (eds) *Of Pots and*

Plans: Papers on the Archaeology and History of Mesopotamia Presented to David Oates in Honour of his 75th Birthday. London, 171–175.

Kuhrt A 1990: "Achaemenid Babylonia: Sources and Problems" in H Sancisi-Weerdenburg & A Kuhrt (eds) *Centre and periphery. Proceedings of the 1986 Achaemenid Workshop.* Achaemenid History IV. (Leiden), 177–194.

Kutscher R 1989: *The Brockmon Tablets at the University of Haifa: Royal Inscriptions.* Haifa.

Laessoe J 1951: "The irrigation system at Ulhu, 8th century BC" (*JCS* 5, 21–32).

Lambert W G 1961: "The Sultantepe Tablets VIII: Shalmaneser in Ararat" (*Anatolian Studies* 11, 143–158).

——2004: "Ištar of Nineveh" (*Iraq* 66, 35–39).

Lanfranchi G B 1995: "Assyrian Geography and Neo-Assyrian Letters; the Location of Hubuškia Again", in M Liverani (ed.) *Neo-Assyrian Geography.* Rome, 127–137.

Layard A H 1853: *Discoveries in the ruins of Nineveh and Babylon.* London.

——1867: *Nineveh and Babylon.* London.

Leichty E 2011: *The Royal Inscriptions of Esarhaddon, King of Assyria (680–669 BC).*

——Royal Inscriptions of the Neo-Assyrian Period, volume 4. Winona Lake.

Livingstone A 1989: *Court Poetry and Literary Miscellanea* (*State Archives of Assyria* III). Helsinki.

Llop J 2008: "MARV 6, 2 und die Eponymfolgen des 12. Jahrhunderts" (*ZA* 98, 20–25).

——2010: "Barley from Alu-ša-Sîn-rabi: Chronological Reflections on an Expedition in the Time of Tukulti-Ninurta I (1233–1197 BC)", in J Vidal (ed.) *Studies on Warfare in the Ancient Near East* (*AOAT* 372), 95–104. Münster.

Luckenbill D D 1924: *The Annals of Sennacherib* (OIP 2). Chicago.

——1927: *Ancient Records of Assyria and Babylonia* (2 volumes). Chicago.

Maeda T 1992: "The Defense Zone During the Rule of the Ur III Dynasty" (*Acta Sumerologica* 14, 135–72).

Mallowan M 1970: "The development of cities from Al-'Ubaid to the end of Uruk 5" (*CAH* I/1, 327–462).

MacGinnis J D A 1988: "A Letter from the *šangû* of Kurbail" (*State Archives of Assyria Bulletin* 2, 67–72).

——2004: "Temple ventures across the river" (*Transeuphratène* 27, 29–35).

——2009: "Erbil Citadel: Archaeological Assessment and Demarcation of Archaeological Zones" in *Revitalisation of Erbil Citadel, Iraq, Phase I: Conservation and Rehabilitation Master Plan.* Volume 1. Technical Report and Rehabilitation Master Plan. UNESCO Ref. No. IRQ/RFP/O8/012: pp. 331–356. Erbil.

——2010: "Mobilisation and Militarisation in the Neo-Babylonian Empire" in J Vidal (ed.) *Studies on Warfare in the Ancient Near East* (*AOAT* 372). Münster, 153–164.

——2013: "Qabra in the cuneiform sources" (*Subartu* [Journal of the Archaeological Syndicate of Kurdistan], vol. 6–7, 1–10).

Machinist P 1982: "Provincial Governance in Middle Assyria and Some New Texts from Yale" (*Assur* 3/2, 1–137).

Matthiae P 1977: *Ebla - An Empire Rediscovered.* London.

Meinhold W 2009: *Ishtar in Assur. Untersuchungen eines Lokalkultes von ca. 2500 bis 614 v. Chr* (AOAT 367). Münster.

Menzel B 1981: *Assyrische Tempel* (2 volumes). Rome.

Miglus P 2003: "Die Siegesstele des Königs Dāduša von Ešnunna und ihre Stellung in der Kunst Mesopotamien und der Nachbargebiete" in R Dittmann, C Eder & B Jacobs (eds) *Altertums Wissenschaften im Dialog: Festschrift für Wolfram Nagel zur Vollendung seines 80. Lebensjahres.* (*AOAT* 306) 397–420.

Millard A 1994: *The Eponyms of the Assyrian Empire, 910–612 BC* (*SAAS* 2). Helsinki.

Nashef K 1982: *Die Orts und Gewässernamen der mittelbabylonischen und mittelassyrischen Zeit.* (*Répertoire Géographiqe des Textes Cunéiformes* 5). Wiesbaden.

Novacek K 2007: Research of the Citadel at Erbil, Kurdistan Region of Iraq, First Season.   Final Report. Plzen.

Novotny J 2008: "Classification of Ashurbanipal's Inscriptions: Prisms C, Kh (+ CND) and G" in R D Biggs, J Meyers & M T Roth (eds) *Proceedings of the 51st Rencontre Assyriologique Internationale, Held at the Oriental Institute of the University of Chicago July 18–22, 2005.* SAOC 22. (Chicago), 127–135.

Oates D 1968: *Studies in the Ancient History of Northern Iraq.* London.

Oded B 1979: *Mass Deportations and Deportees in the Neo-Assyrian Empire.* Wiesbaden.

Parker B 1963: "Economic tablets from the temple of Mamu at Balawat" (*Iraq* 25, 86–103).

Parpola S 1970: *Letters from Assyrian Scholars to the Kings Esarhaddon and Ashurbanipal.* Volume I. Neukirchen-Vluyn.

——1983: *Letters from Assyrian Scholars to the Kings Esarhaddon and Ashurbanipal.* Volume II. Neukirchen-Vluyn.

——2008: "Cuneiform Texts from Ziyaret Tepe (Tušhan), 2002–2003" (*SAAB* 17, 1–137).

Pettinato G 1979: *Catalogo dei testi cuneiformi di Tell Mardikh-Ebla* (Materiali Epigrafici di Ebla, 1). Naples.

Pongratz-Leisten B 1994: *Die Kulttopographische und ideologische Programatik der akītu-Prozessionen in Babylonien und Assyrien im 1. Jahrtausend v. Chr.* (*BaF* 16). Mainz.

Porter, Barbara Nevling 2004: "Ishtar of Nineveh and her collaborator, Ishtar of Arbela, in the reign of Assurbanipal" (*Iraq* 66, 41–44).

Postgate J N 1985: Review of Nashef *RGTC* 5 (*AoF* 32 95–101).

Potts T F 1994: *Mesopotamia and the East. An Archaeological and Historical Study of Foreign Relations ca. 3400–2000 BC.* Cambridge.

Radner K 2006: "Aššur-dūr-pānīya, Statthalter von Til-Barsip inter Sargon II von Assyrien" (*BaM* 37, 185–195).

Reade J E 1964: "More Drawings of Ashurbanipal Sculptures" (*Iraq* 26, 1–13).

——1979: "Narrative Composition in Assyrian Sculpture" (*BaM* 10, 52–110).

Rollinger R 2008: "The 'Median 'Empire', the End of Urartu and Cyrus the Great's Campaign in 547 BC (Nabonidus Chronicle II 16)" (*Ancient West and East* 7, 51–65).

Russell J M 1999: *The Writing on the Wall.* Winona Lake.

Sachs A J 1977: "Achaemenid royal names in Babylonian astronomical texts" (*AJAH* 2, 129–147).

Sachs A J & H Hunger 1988: *Astronomical Diaries and related Texts from Babylonia, volume I: Diaries from 652 BC to 262 BC.* Vienna.

Safar F 1946: "Sennacherib's project for supplying Erbil with water. Part 1" (*Sumer* 2, 50–52).

——1947: "Sennacherib's project for supplying Erbil with water. Part 2" (*Sumer* 3, 23–25).

Saporetti C 1979: *Gli Eponimi Medio-Assiri.* Malibu.

Schmitt R 1991: *The Bisitun Inscriptions of Darius the Great: Old Persian Text.* London.

Shibata D 2007: "Middle Assyrian Administrative and Legal Texts from the 2005 Excavation at Tell Taban: A Preliminary Report" (*Al-Rafidain* 28, 63–74).

Sollberger E & J-R Kupper 1971: *Inscriptions Royales Sumériennes et Akkadiennes.* Paris.

Steinkeller P 1987: "The Administrative and Economic Organization of the Ur III State: The Core and the Periphery" in M Gibson & R Biggs (eds) *The Organization of Power: Aspects of Bureaucracy in the Ancient near East* (Chicago), 19–42.

Streck M 1916: *Ashurbanipal und die letzten Assyrische Könige bis zum Untergange Nineveh's.* Leipzig.

Tavernier J 2007: *Iranica in the Achaemenid Period (ca. 550–330 B.C.): Linguistic Study of Old Iranian Proper Names and Loanwords attested in Non-Iranian Texts* (*OLA* 158). Leuven.

Tenu A 2009: *L'expansion médio-assyrienne: Approche archéologique.* (BAR International Series 1906). Oxford.

Unger E 1928: "Arbailu" (*Reallexicon der Assyriologie* I, 141–142). Berlin.

Ur J 2005: "Sennacherib's northern Assyrian canals: new insights from satellite imagery and aerial photographs" (*Iraq* 67, 317–345).

Vallat F 1993: *Répertoire Géographique des Textes Cunéiformes*. Band 11. Wiesbaden.

Van der Spek R 2003: "Darius III, Alexander the Great and Babylonian Scholarship" in W Henkelman & A Kuhrt (eds) *A Persian Perspective* (*Achaemenid History* XIII), 289–346. Leiden.

Villard P 1995: "Les derniers rapports des devins néo-assyriens" (*RA* 89, 97–107).

Voigtlander E N von 1978: *The Bisitun Inscription of Darius the Great: Babylonian Version* (*Corpus Inscriptionum Iranicarum* Part I volume II). London.

Waetzoldt H 2001: *Wirtschafts- und Verwaltungstexte aus Ebla: Archiv L.2769*. (Materiali Epigrafici di Ebla, 12). Naples.

Walker C B F 1987: *Reading the Past: Cuneiform*. London.

Weidner E 1959: *Die Inschriften Tukulti-Ninurtas I und seiner Nachfolger*. Graz.

Weissbach F H 1911: *Die Keilinschriften der Achämeniden*. Leipzig.

Weissert E 1997: "Royal Hunt and Royal Triumph in a Prism Fragment of Ashurbanipal" in S Parpola & R Whiting (eds) *Assyria 1995* (Helsinki), 339–358.

Wiggermann F A M 1992: *Mesopotamian Protective Spirits: The Ritual Texts*. Groningen.

Wiseman D J 1954: "An Esarhaddon cylinder from Nimrud" (*Iraq* 14, 54–62).

——1955: "Assyrian writing-boards" (*Iraq* 17, 3–13).

Zadok R 1995: "The Ethno-linguistic Character of the Jezireh and Adjacent regions in the 9th–7th Centuries (Assyria Proper vs. Periphery)", in M Liverani (ed.) *Neo-Assyrian Geography*. Rome. 217–282.

Ziegler N 2002: "Le royaume d'Ekallâtum et son horizon géopolitique", in D Charpin & J-M Durand (eds) *Recueil d'études à la mémoire d'André Parrot*, Florilegium Marianum VI, Mémoires de NABU 7. Paris, 211–274.

——2011: "Die Osttigrisregion im Spiegel der Archive von Mari" in P Miglus & S Mühl (eds) *Between the Cultures. The Central Tigris Region from the 3rd to the 1st Millennium BC*. Heidelberger Studien zum Alten Orient 14. Heidelberg, 143–155.